\

SCHWYHART EARLY FAMILY HISTORY

m

Including Ohio, Pennsylvania, Illinois, Iowa, Missouri and more

And Family Connections to the Kinnick and Fletcher, as well as:
Allen – Edick – Gore – Hackett – Hammers – Hamrick –
Hargrove – Hartman – Henton – Hornby – Horton – Jones –
Lewis – Lyon – Marling – Pitts – Richmond – Scott – Seyller –
Tebow – Van Aken – Warden – Wearsch –Weise families

Complied and Researched
by Dr. Bill (William L.) Smith

Table of Contents

Introduction

This book is the second of a series on my mother's line, KINNICK. This book, however, examines and records a unique situation related to the family of my third great-grandmother, Susan SCHWYHART (married Walter KINNICK). After some thorough research on this surname, it has become apparent that the surname derives from two families in the early 1880s where two brothers married two sisters, as explained in Chapter 1.

Chapter 2 is the story of the Walter and Susan (SCHWYHART) KINNICK family from the SCHWYHART perspective. This content is very similar to the comparable family material found in the KINNICK EARLY US FAMILY HISTORY, except it does bring us one full generation closer to the present. The subsequent chapters are siblings and first cousins of Susan, from the two families as explained in Chapter 1.

Some of the content was originally in the "KG Book" – actually a supplement at the end of that book, because Mrs. Waggener really didn't know where our branch fit with the rest of her family. I use the notation "KG book" to refer to the 1953 book: "The Kinnick Family: A Genealogy History of the Kinnick Family of America; Descendants of John Kinnick and Ann Kinnick" by Mrs. Nettie Edna Kinnick Waggener (Mrs. Waggener). Her book was extremely informative relative to the "John and Ann – North Carolina" branch of the family, and also somewhat useful as "family tradition" information for this part. Much new research has been done and added since the KG book was published. This research from census data and other sources, including visits to many counties in Ohio, Indiana, Illinois, Iowa and Kansas, among others, is included here to update the wonderful sources of information in the 1953 book. In the several years leading up to 2003, the fiftieth anniversary of the 1953 book, I compiled the 2003 Kinnick Genealogy Book Online (can be found at: http://freepages.genealogy.rootsweb.ancestry.com/~kinnick/), thanks to the many good folks mentioned herein, and others, in the acknowledgment page at the end of this book.

In addition to vital statistics, for three generations in each Chapter of the book, I have included notes relative to compiled information from others and my own research. These notes range from a simple: "Per KG book" to extensive notes including pension and probate record transcripts, extensive state and federal census notations, or newspaper articles of births, marriages and death/funerals. An example of this range can be seen in Chapter 2, #5, Joseph Kinnick. Note 1 says the KG book has: "Joe Kinnick; no knowledge of his family." By the time you read through Note 7, you have seen a fair review of key elements of his life, from census, family comments, and pension records, among other sources, including a newspaper death notice, followed by detailed listings of all eight of Joseph and Rachel's children.

I owe a special thanks to the materials at and persons associate with the Guernsey County (Ohio) Genealogy Society for the basis of much of my research into the SCHWYHART surname. Thank you to several unknown as well as know contributors there and in other county offices and societies around the country.

All information recorded here should be treated as "family tradition" information. Therefore, you should do your own analysis to prepare a proof of relationships. Where I have reported relationships in this compilation, I feel the reporting is reasonable for me; however, your standard of proof may differ from mine. Pick the parts that interest you, and continue your own family history research. Solving the mysteries is really fun!

I'd love to hear from each of you that read this book. Comments, updates, corrections are welcomed via email at: billsmith2003@gmail.com

Also, other related family history books will continue to be available online at: http://stores.lulu.com/drbillshares

For regular updates, follow my blog at: http://drbillsbookbazaar.blogspot.com/

Chapter 2

First They Were SWINEHEARTs

This book focuses on the two sons of Jacob and Margaret Swineheart, Joseph and Jacob, below, who married sisters, Elizabeth and Sarah Zimmerman, and their families. While these four adults continued to go by Swinehart through their lives, their children all adopted the surname Schwyhart early in their lives and carried it through their lives, and to their descendants.

Before we get to the two families reported, below, I want to take a few words to provide additional background to set these families in their context; information generally beyond the scope of this book. KeyHole (a genealogical publication in Ohio), Vol. XX, No. 1, Jan 1992 (I first read it in Aug 99) refers to the patriarch of the family in America thus:

> Johann Georg Schweinhart, as his name was spelled in German, is given pp. 154-161, as having been the principal in "the first official record found to date which shows that beginning of the German settlement in today's Frederick County."

I found this to be an interesting document in Prince George's County (MD) Court records. Later records show George (born 4 Mar 1681; died 1756 in Frederick County, MD) and Margaret Swinehart. See my additional reporting on this lineage online at:
http://homepages.rootsweb.ancestry.com/~earlyyrs/schwyhartdesc.html

George Swinehart was the grandfather of our Jacob, below, shown as the first generation for this report, through his son, Gabriel (1723-1805).

First Generation

1. **Jacob SWINEHEART** was born about 1746.
Note 1: KeyHole, Vol. XX, No. 1, Jan 1992: Updated family history.... (Aug 99)
On marriage of Henry Z(T)immerman and Catherine Spurgeon on 13 Jan 1825, Jacob Swineheart is listed as brother-in-law.
Note 2: Per Karen Nucci sheets, 8 Sept 1999.
Note 3: Jacob Swinehart is listed in Captain Schockley's Company as a private in the Frontier Rangers in Washington Co, PA, in 17xx.
Note 4: He purchased land in Jefferson Co, OH, in 1806 & 1807.
Note 5: He purchased a plow at a sale in Belmont Co, OH, in 1814.

Jacob SWINEHEART and Margaret UNKNOWN were married about 1775.

Margaret UNKNOWN – additional information sought
Note 1: KeyHole, Vol. XX, No. 1, Jan 1992: Updated family history.... (Aug 99)

Jacob SWINEHEART and Margaret UNKNOWN had the following children:

2   i.   **Gabriel SWINEHART** was born in 1776.

Note 1: KeyHole, Vol. XX, No. 1, Jan 1992: Updated family history....
(Aug 99)
Note 2: He was taxed Belmont Co, OH, 1814.
Note 3: Have birth 1775/1780.

+3 ii. **Elizabeth SWINEHART**, born on 28 Jul 1780; married Solomon HARTMAN, on 28 Oct 1799, Belmont Co, OH; died on 3 Mar 1865, Wayne Co, Ohio.

+4 iii. **Joseph SWINEHEART**, born about 1786, Washington Co, Pennsylvania; married Elizabeth ZIMMERMAN, about 1808; died on 18 Mar 1871, Ohio
   Note 1: Sandi Share, Mar 2006

+5 iv. **Jacob SWINEHEART**, born between 1787 and 1790; married Sarah ZIMMERMAN, on 3 Oct 1814, Belmont Co, Ohio.

+6 v. **Juliann SWINEHART**, born between 1790 and 1795; married Eli LANHAM, on 7 Feb 1815.

7 vi. **John SWINEHART**
   Note 1: KeyHole, Vol. XX, No. 1, Jan 1992: Updated family history....
   (Aug 99)

Second Generation

3. **Elizabeth SWINEHART** (Jacob-1) was born on 28 Jul 1780. She died on 3 Mar 1865 in Wayne Co, Ohio.
Note 1: KeyHole, Vol. XX, No. 1, Jan 1992: Updated family history.... (Aug 99)

Elizabeth SWINEHART and Solomon HARTMAN were married on 28 Oct 1799 in Belmont Co, OH.

Solomon HARTMAN was born on 8 Oct 1778. He died in 1853 in Wayne Co, OH.

Elizabeth SWINEHART and Solomon HARTMAN had the following children:

+8 i. **Adam HARTMAN**, born on 26 Jul 1800.
+9 ii. **Catharine HARTMAN**, born on 16 Jun 1802.
+10 iii. **Phoebe HARTMAN**, born on 18 Aug 1806; died on 3 Jan 1892.
+11 iv. **Elizabeth HARTMAN**, born on 14 May 1821; died on 10 Nov 1900.
+12 v. **Juliana HARTMAN**
13 vi. **John HARTMAN**
14 vii. **Jacob HARTMAN**
15 viii. **Margaret HARTMAN**
16 ix. **Mary HARTMAN**
17 x. **Sarah HARTMAN**
+18 xi. **Rosanna HARTMAN**.
+19 xii. **Delilah HARTMAN**.

4. **Joseph SWINEHEART** (Jacob-1) was born about 1786 in Washington Co, Pennsylvania.

He died on 18 Mar 1871 in Ohio

Note 1: Sandi Share, Mar 2006

Note 2: Listed as Joseph Schwyhart in Knox Township, Guernsey Co, OH in 1820. See Progress Report No. 3, The Kinnick Project [http://www.geocities.com/Heartland/Prairie/4566/kinnick.html]

Note 3: Lived in Belmont Co, OH, in 1817.

Note 4: Listed in the 1827 Enumeration of Belmont County, GRBC (Genealogical Records in Belmont County, Ohio) Volume VII, pp. 65-66: Joseph Swanehart, Jacob Swanetrart, Henry Zimmerman. Obtained at Mid-Continent Library, Jul 2005.

Joseph SWINEHEART and Elizabeth ZIMMERMAN were married about 1808.

Elizabeth ZIMMERMAN (daughter of Henry ZIMMERMAN and Catherine SPURGEON) was born about 1787 in Virginia. She died on 17 Jan 1876 in Belmont Co, OH

Note 1: Sandi Share, Mar 2006

Note 2: Additional information from 1850 census and Knox Township, Guernsey Co, OH records.

Note 3: Per Karen Nucci, Aug 1999, same year of birth, has VA, not OH.

Joseph SWINEHEART and Elizabeth ZIMMERMAN had the following children:

+20	i.	**Susanna (Susan) SCHWYHART**, born on 2 May 1809, Pennsylvania; she first married Walter W. KINNICK, about 1843; after his death, she second married Ephriam YARRINGTON, on 20 Mar 1859; died on 27 Sep 1884.
+21	ii.	**Sarah E. SCHWYHART**, born in 1813; married John Hanson WEEDON, about 20 Apr 1832, Belmont Co, Ohio; died in 1899.
22	iii.	**Barbara SCHWYHART** was born about 1815. Note 1: Same as Maria, m. James Dawson???
+23	iv.	**John SCHWYHART**, born on 16 Jan 1818, Belmont Co, Ohio; married Margaret STONER, about 1835; died on 13 Apr 1883, Adair Co, Iowa.
+24	v.	**Catherine SCHWYHART**, born about 1819/20; married John LEWIS, in 1840; died about 1875.
+25	vi.	**Joseph Z. Jr. SCHWYHART**, born in Sep 1822, Guernsey Co, Ohio; married Rachel Anne MERCER, on 15 Jan 1850, Wheeling Twp, Guernsey Co, Ohio; died on 21 May 1905, Knox Twp, Guernsey Co, Ohio.
+26	vii.	**Jacob SCHWYHART**, born on 6 Aug 1826, Belmont Co, Ohio; married Nancy DUFFEY, on 20 Apr 1848; died on 25 Aug 1885, Wheeling Twp, Guernsey Co, Ohio.
+27	viii.	**William SCHWYHART**, born in Jan 1829, Ohio; married Sophia UNKNOWN, in 1851.
28	ix.	**I. Anderson H. SCHWYHART** was born in 1832 in Ohio. He died before 1882. Note 1: Per 1850 census

5. Jacob SWINEHEART (Jacob-1) was born between 1787 and 1790.

Note 1: KeyHole, Vol. XX, No. 1, Jan 1992: Updated family history.... (Aug 99)

Note 2: Per Karen Nucci, Aug 1999: Marriage date and place.

Note 3: Listed in the 1827 Enumeration of Belmont County, GRBC (Genealogical Records in Belmont County, Ohio) Volume VII, pp. 65-66: Joseph Swanehart, Jacob Swanetrart, Henry Zimmerman. Obtained at Mid-Continent Library, Jul 2005.

Jacob SWINEHEART and Sarah ZIMMERMAN were married on 3 Oct 1814 in Belmont Co, Ohio.

Sarah ZIMMERMAN (daughter of Henry ZIMMERMAN and Catherine SPURGEON) was born in 1792 in Virginia. She died after 1880.
Note 1: KeyHole, Vol. XX, No. 1, Jan 1992: Updated family history.... (Aug 99)
Note 2: Year and State of Birth per Karen Nucci, Aug 1999.
Note 3: In home of daughter Sarah, and her husband, Thomas McKee, in 1880, as Sarah Schuyhart (familysearch.com).

Jacob SWINEHEART and Sarah ZIMMERMAN had the following children:

+29	i.	**Haneh SCHWYHART**, born in 1815, Belmont Co, Ohio; died after 1860.
+30	ii.	**John Z. SCHWYHART**, born in 1817, Ohio.
+31	iii.	**William Z. SCHWYHART**, born in 1821, Belmont Co, Ohio; married Ruth ROBERTS, on 21 Dec 1843, Guernsey Co, Ohio; died in 1862.
+32	iv.	**Sarah SCHWYHART**, born in 1822, Ohio.
+33	v.	**James M. SCHWYHART**, born on 2 Feb 1827, Belmont Co, Ohio; married Susan Matilda BELL, on 8 May 1852, Bellefontaine, Logan Co, Ohio; married Elizabeth OVERSTREET, on 11 Nov 1888, Carroll Co, Arkansas; died on 15 Jul 1900, Stone Co, Missouri.
+34	vi.	**Isaac SCHWYHART**, born on 15 Jul 1829, Belmont Co, Ohio; married Sarah Ann KIMBLE, on 12 Sep 1850; died on 27 May 1862, Camp Shiloh.
35	vii.	**Mary E. SCHWYHART** was born in 1838. Note 1: Per Karen Nucci info 6 Sep 1999

6. **Juliann SWINEHART** (Jacob-1) was born between 1790 and 1795.
Note 1: KeyHole, Vol. XX, No. 1, Jan 1992: Updated family history.... (Aug 99)

Juliann SWINEHART and Eli LANHAM were married on 7 Feb 1815.

Eli LANHAM – additional information sought

Chapter 3

Susan SCHWYHART and Her Descendants

First Generation

1. **Susanna (Susan) SCHWYHART** was born on 2 May 1809 in Pennsylvania. She died on 27 Sep 1884. She was buried in Forest Hill Cemetery, Wyanet, Bureau Co, Illinois.
Note 1: Birthplace: Pennsylvania, per 1850 Census, Bureau Co, IL Birth date: 41 on 1850 census Susan Kinnick again in 1880 census
Note 2: Tombstone inscription, Forest Hill Cemetery, Wyanet, Bureau Co, IL, Lot 258, #2, d. Sep 27, 1884, 75y 4m 25d, name Susanna.
Note 3: Name also SCHWYHART on Fannie (Kinnick) Lyons Marriage Certificate (12-4-95).
Note 4: 1880 census says both her parents also born in PA 1870 census has Susan Yarrington, age 61, Farmer, RE value 960, Personal Estate, value 490, born PA. Also in household, Jacob, age 24, Eveline Harrison, age 15, Mary Harrison, age 13, in Concord area of Bureau County.
Note 5: Listed in the 1827 Enumeration of Belmont County, GRBC (Genealogical Records in Belmont County, Ohio) Volume VII, pp. 65-66: Joseph Swanehart, Jacob Swanetrart, Henry Zimmerman. Obtained at Mid-Continent Library, Jul 2005.

Susanna (Susan) SCHWYHART married Walter W. KINNICK about 1843 – still seeking details.

Walter W. KINNICK (son of John KINNICK and Mary ISAAC) was born on 11 Feb 1810 in Maryland. He died on 28 Feb 1853. He was buried in Forest Hill Cemetery, Wyanet, Bureau Co, Illinois.
Note 1: Birthplace: Maryland, per 1850 Census, Bureau Co, Dover, IL. Birth date: 41 on 1850 Census
Note 2: From children's birthdates in 1850 census, appeared to have lived in Ohio from before 1835 until1843 or 1850.
Note 3: Walter birth per Kinnick 1953 genealogy book
Note 4: Died before 1860 (actually before 3-20-1859 when Susan remarried), in Concord twp., Bureau Co., IL 1840 Belmont Co, Ohio; 1860-80 Bureau Co, IL census data
Note 5: Tombstone inscription, Forest Hill Cemetery, Wyanet, Bureau Co, IL, Lot 258, #1, d. Feb 28, 1853, 43y, 17d

Susanna (Susan) SCHWYHART and Walter W. KINNICK had the following children:

+2	i.	**Mary E. KINNICK**, born about 1835, Ohio; died before 1869.
+3	ii.	**Sarah Ann KINNICK**, born in Apr 1836, Ohio; married Thomas RICHMOND, on 11 Feb 1854, Bureau Co, Illinois; died about 1914.
4	iii.	**John S. KINNICK** was born in 1837 in Ohio. He died on 5 Jun 1851. He was buried in Forest Hill Cemetery, Wyanet, Bureau Co, Illinois. Note 1: 1850 census: death and marital (unmarried) status per 1953 KG book, says killed in action, Civil War, about 1865 - but, see below!

Note 2: Tombstone inscription, Forest Hill Cemetery, Wyanet, Bureau Co, IL, Lot 258, #3, d. Jun 5, 1851, 16y, 9m, 22d. Therefore, birth date = 14 Sep 1834 ?? or should it be 1837?

Note 3: John was listed in order of the children as age 13, in the 1850 census, that would be born in 1837, between Sarah and Joseph.

Note 4: This is also confirmed by the 1840 census. Will want to check on whether the age 16 on the tombstone inscription could be a 14.

+5   iv.   **Joseph KINNICK**, born on 9 Mar 1839, Belmont Co, Ohio; married Rachel Ann MERCER, on 29 Feb 1860, Bureau Co, Illinois; died on 24 Sep 1917, Park City, Stillwater Co, Montana.

+6   v.   **Walter Watson KINNICK**, born on 11 Nov 1840, Belmont Co, Ohio; married Mary Estelle SIMMONS, on 6 Feb 1862; died on 10 Mar 1919, Buda, Illinois.

+7   vi.   **Catharine KINNICK**, born on 20 Apr 1842, Ohio; married John Thomas FLETCHER, in Mar 1859, Bureau Co, Illinois; died on 30 Mar 1927.

8   vii.   **William KINNICK** was born on 2 Feb 1844 in Ohio. He died in Oct 1845 in Illinois.

Note 1: Details from Evelyn L. McKittrick, 10 Sep 1996.

+9   viii.   **Jacob KINNICK**, born on 4 Jan 1846, Bureau Co, Illinois; married Hattie VANDRAM, on 25 Nov 1867; married Fanny FLETCHER, on 28 Apr 1872, Bureau Co, Illinois; died on 6 Mar 1923, Wyanet, Bureau Co, Illinois.

+10   ix.   **Margaret (Maggie) KINNICK**, born on 2 Feb 1851, Princeton Twp, Bureau Co, Illinois; married Jacob E. WEISE, in Sep 1871, Bureau Co, Illinois; died on 19 Feb 1903, at home, Wyanet, Bureau Co, Illinois.

+11   x.   **Fanny Susan KINNICK**, born on 1 Nov 1851, Bureau Co, Illinois; married William Eugene LYON, on 30 Dec 1879, Buda, Bureau Co, Illinois; died on 18 Feb 1926, Ohio Twp, Ness Co, Kansas.

Susanna (Susan) SCHWYHART second married Ephriam YARRINGTON on 20 Mar 1859. It was a second marriage for each.

Ephriam YARRINGTON was born about 1802 in Pennsylvania. He died on 24 Feb 1870 in Princeton, Bureau Co, Illinois.

Note 1: All details to 25 Nov 1995 on E Yarrington; from E. Marsh letter.

Second Generation

2. **Mary E. KINNICK** (Susanna (Susan) SCHWYHART-1) was born about 1835 in Ohio. She died before 1869.

Note 1: 1850 census

George W. HARRISON – additional information sought

Note 1: Per Chancery Records, Bureau Co, IL, General Docket - Term #73 General #1484, 23 Nov 1869.

Note 2: Fletcher "family tradition" notes say Joe Harrison, per details from Evelyn L.

McKittrick, 10 Sep 1996.

Mary E. KINNICK and George W. HARRISON had the following children:

+12   i.   **Eveline HARRISON**, born on 21 Dec 1854, Wyanet, Bureau Co, Illinois; married Francis (Frank) HORNBY, on 22 Jan 1876, Illinois; died on 2 Jan 1934, at home, Estherville, Emmet Co, Iowa.

13   ii.   **Mary A. HARRISON** was born on 9 Nov 1856 in Bureau Co, Illinois. She died on 12 Apr 1880. She was buried in Forest Hill Cemetery, Wyanet, Bureau Co, Illinois.
Note 1: 1860 Census said Mary S., tombstone says Mary A.
Note 2: Tombstone inscription, Forest Hill Cemetery, Wyanet, Bureau Co, IL, Lot 45, #9, Mary A. Harrison, d. Apr 12, 1880, 23y, 5 m, 21d.
Note 3: 1870 census has Mary, age 13, with grandmother, Susan

3. **Sarah Ann KINNICK** (Susanna (Susan) SCHWYHART-1) was born in Apr 1836 in Ohio. She died about 1914.
Note 1: 1850 census; middle name and marriage info from 1953 KG book.
Note 2: Marriage date, WS#2, 11-2-95, from Illinois Marriage Index Project.
Note 3: Per Jet Hall 27 Nov 95 Info, birth and death dates
Note 4: 1900 census has her living with son Aron in Concord Twp, Bureau Co, born Apr 1836, Div. (says mother of 2 children, both living?! s/b 6!)
Note 5: 1870 census has Sarah with Thomas and kids at age 33, farming in Concord, Sheffield Post Office.
Note 6: 1880 census, Sarah A., age 44, divorced, with 3 kids.
Note 7: 1910 census, age 74, living with son John W and family; Concord Township, county road; 8 children, 5 living, widowed?
Note 8: Mazie (Fletcher) Ross comment, rec'd from Violet Lowe, 8-23-96: I remember Aunt Sarah Ann (Grandma Fletcher Sister). She had one glass eye. Something flew in her eye when she was shaking the rug.

Sarah Ann KINNICK and Thomas RICHMOND were married on 11 Feb 1854 in Bureau Co, Illinois.

Thomas RICHMOND was born about 1835 in Iowa. He died about 1910.
Note 1: Died before 1923
Note 2: Per Jet Hall 27 Nov 95 Info, birth and death dates
Note 3: Daughter Sarah, in 1910 census, says father born in Iowa. 1900 census of son, Aron, says father born in Canada!
Note 4: 1870 and 1880 census, him and kids, say he born in Canada. Divorced prior to 1880, did not find him in 1880 census.

Sarah Ann KINNICK and Thomas RICHMOND had the following children:

+14   i.   **Almira RICHMOND**, born about 1855; married Delos LAY, in 1877; died about 1918.

15   ii.   **William RICHMOND** was born on 11 Jun 1857. He died on 19 Mar 1858.

He was buried in Forest Hill Cemetery, Wyanet, Bureau Co, Illinois.
Note 1: Per Jet Hall 27 Nov 95 Info, existence, birth and death dates
Note 2: Exact birth and death dates from Forest Hill Cemetery, Wyanet

+16   iii. **Sarah RICHMOND**, born in Oct 1860, Missouri; died on 13 Mar 1935
Note 1: Illinois Statewide Death Index, 1916-1950: Sarah Ann Hackett, female, white, age 74, Cert# 12795, 13 March 1935, Whiteside County, City: Tampico.

+17   iv. **Laura A. RICHMOND**, born on 24 Jul 1862, Bureau Co, Illinois; married Francis Newton (F. N.) SCOTT, on 3 Sep 1879, Bureau Co, Illinois; died on 11 Jul 1905, Allison, Butler Co, IA.

+18   v. **Frances Belle (Belle) RICHMOND**, born about 1865; died about 1895.

+19   vi. **John W. RICHMOND**, born in Nov 1867, Illinois; married Lydia Ann II HALL, about 1892; died about 1939.

+20   vii. **Aron I. RICHMOND**, born in Dec 1869; died after 1923.

21   viii. **Frank E. RICHMOND** was born on 4 Nov 1872. He died on 26 Aug 1874. He was buried in Forest Hill Cemetery, Wyanet, Bureau Co, Illinois.
Note 1: Per Jet Hall 27 Nov 95 Info, existence, birth and death dates
Note 2: Exact birth and death dates from Forest Hill Cemetery, Wyanet

5. **Joseph KINNICK** (Susanna (Susan) SCHWYHART-1) was born on 9 Mar 1839 in Belmont Co, Ohio. He died on 24 Sep 1917 in Park City, Stillwater Co, Montana.
Note 1: 1850 census; 1953 KG book says: Joe Kinnick; no knowledge of his family; married; 2 sons and 4 daughters.
Note 2: 1860 census, Concord Twp, Bureau Co, Joseph listed at age 22 as farmer, separately, as part of Carrington household, with female also age 22, presumably wife, name Amelia (?); (both born in Ohio)
Note 3: Marcella Mickel 1978 letter, based on GSA pension papers (presumably) says birth year was 1839, lists eight children. Also says born in Richland or Belmont Co (why Richland??). Also says: Co D, 7th Reg, Kan Cavalry!! Death place: Park City, Stillwater Co, Montana; farmer, Civil War.
Note 4: From Marcella Mickel: Rock Island, 14 March 1865: "a little daughter of Mrs. KINNICK, living about 6 miles above Sheffield in Bureau County, died in a fire last Thursday aged about 5 y. She was alone in the home at the time with another child, aged 18m. Mr. Kinnick is a soldier." This appears to be Amanda who died, the younger sister is Margaret. Joseph was mustered out of the Civil War service in St. Louis on 10 March 1865.
Note 5: Mazie (Fletcher) Ross comment, rec'd from Violet Lowe, 8-23-96: I remember Uncle Joe and Aunt Rachel (Grandma Fletcher brother and his wife) Uncle Walt, Uncle Jake and Aunt Fannie. (These were Grandma's brother and Fannie was Grandpa's sister)
Note 6: Pension File, Cert. No. 942830, statement dated 22 Apr 1909, lists places of residence since leaving service: Bureau Co, IL until 1872; Madison Co, IA until 1877; Adair Co, IA until 1886; Des Moines, IA until 1888; Yellowstone Co, MT since. Current post office is Huntley, Montana. Personal description on "Declaration for Pension" has: Height, 5 feet, 11 1/2 inches; complexion, Dark; color of eyes, Brown; color of hair, black; occupation, farmer.
Note 7: 1900 Federal census - Montana, Yellowstone Co, Park City Precinct: Joseph and Rachel, with son, George.
Note 8: Civil War Service: Co D, 7 Kan Cavalry
Note 9: Joseph Kinnick Household, 1900 U. S. Census, population schedule, Montana,

Yellowstone County, Park City Precinct, p. 6A, dwelling 122, family 130. Joseph Kinnick, head, male, born March 1839, age 61, married forty years, born in Ohio, father born in Maryland, mother born in Ohio, occupation: Farmer. Rachel Kinnick, wife, female, born May 1839, age 61, married forty years, seven children, five living, born in Ohio, father born in Ohio, mother born in Ohio. George Kinnick, son, male, born August 1878, age 21, single, born in Iowa, both parents born in Ohio, occupation: Sheep Shearer.

Note 10: Wm. MERCER an old settler on the Blue died Thursday. His son-in-law and family, Joseph KINNICK of Montana were here. Source: AURORA SUN 29 September 1900; extracted from: http://www.rootsweb.com/~nesgs/Ancestree/vol10/v10n01p23.htm, after a Google search for Joseph Kinnick, May 2005. Nebraska State Genealogical Society Journals, NEBRASKA ANCESTREE, Volume X, no. 1- Summer 1987.

Joseph KINNICK and Rachel Ann MERCER were married on 29 Feb 1860 in Bureau Co, Illinois.

Rachel Ann MERCER (daughter of William MERCER and Mary FLETCHER) was born on 15 Mar 1839 in Harrison Co, Ohio. She died on 10 Dec 1917. She was buried on 12 Dec 1917 in Park City, Stillwater Co, Montana.

Note 1: Birth date and place, death estimate from Marcella Mickel 1978 letter

Note 2: Grandson Mark Edick has GM Rachel N, age 84 (?), on 1920 census, Park Co., MT. Appears to be paternal grandmother, not maternal (8-17-96)

Note 3: Per Marcella Mickel letter to S.B. 1 Apr 1984, Rachel Ann (Mercer) Kinnick, died 10 Dec 1917, Park City, Stillwater Co, MT, just three months after her husband, Joseph.

Note 4: 1900 Federal census - Montana, Yellowstone Co, Park City Precinct: with Joseph and son, George, age 21; married 40 years, 7 children, 5 living. I have 8 children - ??

Joseph KINNICK and Rachel Ann MERCER had the following children:

22	i.	**Amanda Elenora KINNICK** was born on 23 Nov 1860 in Bureau Co, Illinois. She died in Mar 1865 in Sheffield, Bureau Co, Illinois. Note 1: Died before 1923, per Jacob estate. Note 2: From Marcella Mickel: Rock Island, 14 March 1865: "a little daughter of Mrs. KINNICK, living about 6 miles above Sheffield in Bureau County, died in a fire last Thursday aged about 5 y. She was alone in the home at the time with another child, aged 18m. Mr. Kinnick is a soldier." This appears to be Amanda who died, the younger sister is Margaret. Joseph was mustered out of the Civil War service in St. Louis on 10 March 1865.
+23	ii.	**Margaret Susana (Maggie) KINNICK**, born on 5 Jan 1863, Bureau Co, Illinois; married William H. (Bill) EDICK, on 13 Apr 1882, Greenfield, Adair Co, Iowa; died on 23 Aug 1951, Mill Creek, Park County, Montana.
+24	iii.	**William Walter KINNICK**, born on 15 Mar 1866, Bureau Co, Illinois; married Guadelupe Ramono COVURRUBIAS, in 1907/8; married Lilian UNKNOWN, in 1897; died on 17 Apr 1946, Livingston, Montana.
+25	iv.	**John Leach Cook KINNICK**, born on 22 Mar 1868, near, Buda, Bureau Co, Illinois; married Ida Elizabeth (Lizzie) MCAFERTY, on 25 Sep 1890, Billings, Yellowstone Co, Montana; died on 7 May 1935, Laurel, Stillwater Co, Montana.

| +26 | v. | **Mary Eppenetes (Mate) KINNICK**, born on 23 May 1870, Bureau Co, Illinois; died between 1947 and 1949. |
| 27 | vi. | **Joseph Ernest KINNICK** was born on 1 May 1874 in Madison Co, Iowa. He died before 1897. |

Note 1: He died before 1923, no children surviving, per Jacob estate info.
Note 2: Not living, 22 Oct 1897, per pension file.
Note 3: Sketch on William Walter says he had a brother, "Ernest, who died as a young man .." Probably the same person.

| 28 | vii. | **Jessie H. KINNICK** was born on 5 Apr 1875 in Madison Co, Iowa. She died before 1897. |

Note 1: He died before 1923, no children surviving, per Jacob estate.
Note 2: Not living, 22 Oct 1897, per pension file.

| +29 | viii. | **George Butler KINNICK**, born on 2 Aug 1878, Adair Co, Iowa; married Belle Winnie HOLMES, in 1905; died on 27 Oct 1972, Fort Lauderdale, Broward Co, Florida. |

6. **Walter Watson KINNICK** (Susanna (Susan) SCHWYHART-1) was born on 11 Nov 1840 in Belmont Co, Ohio. He died on 10 Mar 1919 in Buda, Illinois. He was buried in Hopeland Cemetery, Buda, Illinois.

Note 1: Gravestone says Veteran 61-65; have veteran' record from wife obit and Kansas Reg files.
Note 2: Per 1910 census, living with Lee and Margaret Brewer, age 69, Own Income, Union Army veteran, widowed.
Note 3: 1900 census has Walter, age 59, Day Laborer, with Mary, age 56, and Etta, age 15, and Grace, age 12.
Note 4: Mazie (Fletcher) Ross comment, rec'd from Violet Lowe, 8-23-96: I remember Uncle Joe and Aunt Rachel (Grandma Fletcher brother and his wife) Uncle Walt, Uncle Jake and Aunt Fannie. (These were Grandma's brother and Fannie was Grandpa's sister)
Note 5: 1870 census has Walter, Mary E, Erastus, Emma, and Margaret in Harrison Twp, Adair Co, IA, Dexter P.O., near the Van Akens and Alonzo P. Edick family. Walter and Mary E become the parents of a son, Alonzo P., there during 1870. Census was 28 Jul, Alonzo born in nearby Stuart, 2 Nov 1870. (1870 census, Adair Co, Iowa, Index: http://ftp.rootsweb.com/pub/usgenweb/ia/adair/census/1870/ad70indx.txt)

Walter Watson KINNICK and Mary Estelle SIMMONS were married on 6 Feb 1862.

Mary Estelle SIMMONS (daughter of George SIMMONS and Mary Elizabeth LEE) was born on 8 Aug 1843 in Bureau Co, Illinois. She died on 7 Jan 1909 in Will Carper home, Buda, Bureau Co, Illinois. She was buried on 10 Jan 1909 in Hopeland Cemetery, Buda, Bureau Co, Illinois.

Note 1: Gravestone says born Aug 8, 1843, died Jan 7, 1909.
Note 2: Have Obituary, 11/16/95.
Note 3: She accompanied Walter to Civil War, in Corinth, Miss.
Note 4: 1900 census has Walter, age 59, Day Laborer, with Mary, age 56, and Etta, age 15, and Grace, age 12.

Walter Watson KINNICK and Mary Estelle SIMMONS had the following children:

30	i.	**Joseph Erastus KINNICK** was born on 13 Nov 1864 in Buda, Illinois. He died on 27 Jul 1925.

30   i.   **Joseph Erastus KINNICK** was born on 13 Nov 1864 in Buda, Illinois. He died on 27 Jul 1925.

Note 1: Listed in his mother's obit, 1909, as Erastus Kinnick, (first son).

Note 2: Listed as Erastus in estate of his brother Jacob in 1923, living in Stalwart, Saskatchewan, Canada. Listed in 1900 as Erastus, living with Alonzo in Coon Rapids, farm hand, said age 34, birth in Nov 65 (rather than 64 we have from KG).

Note 3: In 1880 census, listed as Joseph Kinnick, age 15, IL, Farm Labor, in home of Frank Hornby, cousin; Concord, Bureau Co, IL (Family Search files).

Note 4: In Canadian Census of 1911, he is in Regina, Saskatchewan.

31   ii.   **Nora E. KINNICK** was born on 4 Jan 1866 in Buda, Bureau Co, Illinois. She died on 10 Feb 1866 in Buda, Bureau Co, Illinois. She was buried in Hopeland Cemetery, Buda, Illinois.

Note 1: Birth and Death Dates from Gravestone, 1995.

+32   iii.   **Emma Estella KINNICK**, born on 9 Dec 1866, Buda, Bureau Co, Illinois; married William S. (Will) CARPER, in Jan 1894, Buda, Bureau Co, Illinois; died on 4 Mar 1935.

+33   iv.   **Margaret Ann (Maggie) KINNICK**, born on 7 Dec 1868, Buda, Bureau Co, Illinois; married Lee BREWER, in Jan 1891, Buda, Bureau Co, Illinois; died on 10 Feb 1920, Buda, Bureau Co, Illinois.

+34   v.   **Alonzo Palmer KINNICK**, born on 2 Nov 1870, Stuart, Adair Co, Iowa; married Margaret Jeanette (Nettie) WILLIAMS, on 6 Jul 1891, Carroll, Carroll Co, Iowa; died on 27 Feb 1923, Coon Rapids, Carroll Co, Iowa.

35   vi.   **George Walter KINNICK** was born on 18 Sep 1872 in Mendon, Missouri. He died on 18 Dec 1942.

Note 1: George noted as in Idaho in "Buda" book, see Katie.

Note 2: Living in Inkum, ID, c/o O.A. Scott. in 1923, per Jacob Estate. WWI Civilian Draft Registrations (Ancestry.com) Walter George   18 Sep brother lives Coon Kinnick   1872   White   Rapids IA   Power Idaho

Note 3: From obituary of Mary Etta Kinnick Horton, died 6 December 1939, under survivors: "George Kinnick, Dixon, Montana."

+36   vii.   **Ira Odell KINNICK**, born on 20 Jul 1874, Buda, Bureau Co, Illinois; married Delta Mae MCCOY, on 26 Nov 1913.

+37   viii.   **Katherine Susan (Katie) KINNICK**, born on 22 Feb 1876, Buda, Bureau Co, Illinois; married Levi HAMRICK, on 26 Jun 1895, Kinnick home, Buda, Bureau Co, Illinois; died on 20 Jan 1929, Greeley, Colorado.

38   ix.   **Fanny Alice KINNICK** was born on 13 Mar 1878 in Buda, Bureau Co, Illinois. She died on 26 May 1894 in parent's home, Buda, Bureau Co, Illinois. She was buried on 28 May 1894 in Hopeland Cemetery, Buda, Illinois.

Note 1: Date of Death from Gravestone, 1995.

Note 2: Have Bureau Co Republican article from May 31. Baptist services described in some detail! W/Bureau Co report # 6.

39   x.   **John KINNICK** was born on 6 Nov 1880 in Buda, Bureau Co, Illinois. He

died on 18 Nov 1881 in Buda, Bureau Co, Illinois. He was buried in Hopeland Cemetery, Buda, Illinois.
Note 1: Listed as John on Gravestone, not Johnny as in KG book.

+40 xi. **Mary Etta KINNICK**, born on 17 May 1885, Buda, Bureau Co, Illinois; married Simon Garfield (Garfield) HORTON, on 31 Dec 1902, Buda, Bureau Co, Illinois; died on 6 Dec 1939.

+41 xii. **Gracie Irene KINNICK**, born on 30 Oct 1887, Buda, Bureau Co, Illinois; married John SEYLLER, in Jan 1907, Buda, Bureau Co, Illinois; died on 29 Dec 1945.

7. **Catharine KINNICK** (Susanna (Susan) SCHWYHART-1) was born on 20 Apr 1842 in Ohio. She died on 30 Mar 1927. She was buried in New Cemetery, Crawfordsville, Washington Co, Iowa.
Note 1: 1850 census lists as Catherine, age 8, born in Ohio 1953 KG book lists: Kate (Katherine) Kinnick Fletcher, married William Fletcher; 5 sons and 4 daughters.
Note 2: Catherine on Wedding Doc., and says John Fletcher rather than Wm.(1859).
Note 3: William not correct, married John T. per many records in Bureau Co report #4, including census
Note 4: Jacob estate settlement says she lived in Crawsfordsville, Washington Co, IA in 1923.
Note 5: 1880 census, Concord twp, John T, 47y, Catherine, 36y (b. 1844), age 26 on 1870 census. Will use 1850 census, born 1842, spelled Catharine (12/17/95); in Obit of Ora L, it says Katherine Kinnick Fletcher!!

Catharine KINNICK and John Thomas FLETCHER were married in Mar 1859 in Bureau Co, Illinois.

John Thomas FLETCHER (son of Townsend FLETCHER and Susannah (Susan) READY) was born on 14 Mar 1833 in Virginia. He died on 22 Jan 1920 in Washington Co, Iowa. He was buried in New Cemetery, Crawfordsville, Washington Co, Iowa.
Note 1: Age 16 on 1850 census, among father's children
Note 2: J T Fletcher on 1920 Soundex, age 86, born in VA! Wife, Kathren, 77, Nellie 39 and Grace 32. Fits with Ora L. obit from 1937!! 1-27-96.
Note 3: Appears family moved to Iowa right after his mother died in Nov 1887 and before Grace born in Iowa in 1888!.
Note 4: 1900 Soundex, IA, Washington Co, Crawfordsville Twp., John T. age 67, b. VA, Kathrin, born Apr 1842, age 58 (b. OH), with Frank, Nellie, Clark and Grace.
Note 5: John Thomas F. per Death Record/Obit 1870 census says age 36, 1880 says age 47. Farmer; also, 1870 census has Susan, age 78, and, Fannie, age 38.

Catharine KINNICK and John Thomas FLETCHER had the following children:

+42 i. **Fannie Elizabeth FLETCHER**, born on 21 Jul 1860, Illinois; married John E. WILLIAMS, on 28 Feb 1888, Washington Co, Iowa; died on 30 Jan 1930.

43 ii. **Susie E. FLETCHER** was born on 29 May 1862 in Illinois. She died on 25 Feb 1879 in Bureau Co, Illinois. She was buried in Forest Hill Cemetery, Wyanet, Bureau Co, Illinois.

Note 1: Per Forest Hill Cemetery info, died 25 Feb 1879, 16y, 10m, 27d Bureau County Republican, Thursday, March 6, 1879: "Susan, daughter of John Fletcher, aged 17 years, was buried last week Wednesday of diphtheria." Obtained with Report 5, Bureau Co.

Note 2: 1870 census has Susan, age 8. Fannie age 10. Jno age 6

Note 3: Birth date per Violet letter 18 Mar 1996.

+44   iii. **John Townsend (Jack) FLETCHER**, born on 28 Nov 1863, near Sheffield, Concord Twp, Bureau Co, Illinois; married Carrie May WHYTE, on 3 Oct 1888, Crawfordsville, Washington Co, Iowa; married Laura WILES, on 10 Jan 1914; died on 30 Jun 1931, at home, Crawfordsville, Washington Co, Iowa.

45   iv. **James Willard FLETCHER** was born on 9 Feb 1866 in Bureau Co, Illinois. He died on 18 Mar 1951 in University Hosp, Iowa City, Johnson Co, Iowa. He was buried in New Cemetery, Crawfordsville, Washington Co, Iowa.

Note 1: Per 1880 Census, Concord Twp, Bureau Co, IL

Note 2: James lives in Iowa in 1937 when Ora L. died.

Note 3: On 1900 Concord Co census, there is a James Fletcher, age 34, b. Feb 1866, living as laborer in home of Alvin Miller. Single, born in IL, parents born OH, OH. Fits except his father born in VA, would he know?

Note 4: 1870 census has Jas age 3; 1880 census has James W. age 13.

Note 5: Per obit, James was reared and educated in IL. He moved to the Crawfordsville community in 1883 and had been engaged in farming and tiling there. He had tiled many of the farms in the Welsh neighborhoods.

Note 6: Apparently never married.

Note 7: Middle name from Evelyn L. McKittrick, 10 Sep 1996.

+46   v. **Edna Evelyn FLETCHER**, born on 6 Nov 1869, Bureau Co, Illinois; married Charles Franklin (Frank) HULL, on 25 Jan 1893, Iowa; died on 28 Oct 1946, County Hospital, Washington, Washington Co, Iowa.

+47   vi. **Royal W. FLETCHER**, born on 3 Oct 1872, Sheffield, Illinois; married Alice GRIFFITH, on 18 Jun 1891, Washington Co, Iowa; died about Dec 1948.

+48   vii. **Ora Layton FLETCHER**, born on 20 Oct 1874, Hickory Grove, Illinois; married Rose Ella HALL, on 19 Dec 1900; died on 29 Jul 1937, Gold Twp, Bureau Co, Illinois.

+49   viii. **Samuel Clinton (Clint) FLETCHER**, born on 19 Jan 1877, Bureau Co, Illinois; married Delia Anna HULL, on 19 Dec 1900, Muscatine, Iowa; died on 22 Oct 1953, Crawfordsville, Washington Co, Iowa.

+50   ix. **Frank William FLETCHER**, born on 9 Dec 1878, Bureau Co, Illinois; married Jessie Luella MITCHELL, on 6 Feb 1907, Crawfordsville, Washington Co, Iowa; died on 5 Mar 1955, University Hosp, Iowa City, Johnson Co, Iowa.

51   x. **Nellie E. FLETCHER** was born on 19 Dec 1880 in Bureau Co, Illinois. She died on 10 Oct 1955 in at home, Crawfordsville, Washington Co, Iowa. She was buried in New Cemetery, Crawfordsville, Washington Co, Iowa.

Note 1: Nellie lived in Iowa in 1937, when Ora L. died; first knowledge of her.

Note 2: Obit says twelve siblings. One brother and two sisters preceded Ora.
Note 3: Name, age and birth date and place confirmed by 1920 Soundex 1-27-96.
Note 4: 1900 census says Nellie E, Dec 1881.
Note 5: Obit says 19 Dec 1890, s/b 1880, in IL, not IA in 1890. She was reared and educated in Crawfordsville and had lived in the county for 70 years; a member of the Methodist church.

+52   xi.   **Clark Eugene FLETCHER**, born on 6 May 1883, Bureau Co, Illinois; married Mame CHERRYHOLMES, on 11 Apr 1906, Crawfordsville, Washington Co, Iowa; died on 16 Feb 1966.

53   xii.   **Grace A. FLETCHER** was born on 14 Dec 1887 in near, Crawfordsville, Washington Co, Iowa. She died on 13 Sep 1971 in Rest Haven NH, Mt. Pleasant, Iowa. She was buried in New Cemetery, Crawfordsville, Washington Co, Iowa.
Note 1: Grace lived in Iowa in 1937, when Ora L. died; first knowledge of her.
Note 2: Obit says twelve siblings. One brother and two sisters preceded Ora.
Note 3: Name, age and birth date and place confirmed by 1920 Soundex 1-27-96.
Note 4: 1900 census says Grace A., born Dec 1887, IA.
Note 5: Her obit: She was reared in that community and had taught school for a number of years. She was a member of the Methodist church. The last of a family of 12 children, she is survived by a number of nieces and nephews.

9. **Jacob KINNICK** (Susanna (Susan) SCHWYHART-1) was born on 4 Jan 1846 in Bureau Co, Illinois. He died on 6 Mar 1923 in Wyanet, Bureau Co, Illinois.
Note 1: 1850 census (and age 14 in 1869 census); 1953 KG book: Jake (Jacob) Kinnick, no family, m Fanny Fletcher; no children.
Note 2: Birth 4 Jan 1846 based on death certificate 7 Mar 1923, IL, 77 yr, 2 mo, 2 da.
Note 3: On Sec 11, Wyanet in 1877.
Note 4: Have Will and Probate record copies.
Note 5: Divorced Harriet (Hattie) in 1872.
Note 6: He was living 1880 in Concord twp, Bureau Co, IL (see details in Fannie)
Note 7: In 1870 census, with mother Susan, on farm, Concord area of Bureau County, age 24, working on farm; Eveline and Mary Harrison, also.
Note 8: 1900 Census has Jacob, age 54, married 28 years, no children, to Fanny, age 66. Also in household, Ora L Fletcher, age 25, as Boarder, along with an 11 year old, Forest Ready. Ready is family name of Fanny's mother.
Note 9: 1910 census has Jacob J, age 64, Farmer, with Fannie, age 77, and family of Ora Fletcher, wife, Rose, and children, Earl and Inez.
Note 10: Mazie (Fletcher) Ross comment, rec'd from Violet Lowe, 8-23-96: I remember Uncle Joe and Aunt Rachel (Grandma Fletcher brother and his wife) Uncle Walt, Uncle Jake and Aunt Fannie. (These were Grandma's brother and Fannie was Grandpa's sister) Uncle Jake and Aunt Fannie raised Uncle Ora - Aunt Fannie made me a book from Sunday School papers. Aunt Rachel was a Seventh Day Adventist. She wrote poems.
Note 11: Civil War Service: Co. H, 146 IL Infantry.

Jacob KINNICK and Hattie VANDRAM were married on 25 Nov 1867. They were divorced.

Hattie VANDRAM – little is know of her – more information sought.

Jacob KINNICK second married Fanny FLETCHER on 28 Apr 1872 in Bureau Co, Illinois.

Fanny FLETCHER (daughter of Townsend FLETCHER and Susannah (Susan) READY) was born about 1832 in Fauquier Co, Virginia. She died on 24 Mar 1920 in Gold Twp, Bureau Co, IL. She was buried in Forest Hill Cemetery, Wyanet, Bureau Co, Illinois.
Note 1: Per Jet Hall 27 Nov 95 Info, birth and death dates
Note 2: In 1880 census: Jacob, 84y (reading error, is 34!); Fannie, 40y (reporting error, is 48!); also in household, Lovina Weeden, niece, 16y, going to school; Susan Fletcher, 82y, Mother-in law; Susan Kinnick, 71y, Mother. (all relationships to Jacob, as HOH, of course)
Note 3: In 1870 Census, Fannie Fletcher, age 38, living with brother and sister-in-law, John T. and Catherine Fletcher, and family; married Jacob Kinnick in 1872.
Note 4: Francis, age 17, on 1850 census, kids in order!
Note 5: WS#1, Death record #2391 (1920); same date on Forest Hill, Wyanet, Cemetery records, b. 1832
Note 6: Death date from Illinois Statewide Death Index (on-line), 1916-1950 - also had Jacob, Wyanet - only Kinnicks listed!

10. **Margaret (Maggie) KINNICK** (Susanna (Susan) SCHWYHART-1) was born on 2 Feb 1851 in Princeton Twp, Bureau Co, Illinois. She died on 19 Feb 1903 in at home, Wyanet, Bureau Co, Illinois. She was buried on 20 Feb 1903 in Forest Hill Cemetery, Wyanet, Bureau Co, Illinois.
Note 1: 1850 census age 3/12; 1953 KG book: Margaret Kinnick Wise, m Jacob Wise; 2 sons.
Note 2: Listed as age 10 on 1860 census.
Note 3: Death date about 1903 from county clerk, see WS#2, 11-22-95. In view of this, the infant Wise buried in Hopeland is probably a grandson.
Note 4: WS#6, death certificate, Wise, age 52 years 18 day.; Cemetery spells name Weise, as does newspaper.!! Death notice in paper; says born in Princeton Twp
Note 5: WS# 6: The newspaper says died at home two miles west of Wyanet; leaves husband and two sons, three brothers and three sisters (Joseph, Walter, Jacob; Sarah, Catherine, Fanny).

Margaret (Maggie) KINNICK and Jacob E. WEISE were married in Sep 1871 in Bureau Co, Illinois.

Jacob E. WEISE (son of John Trimmer WISE and Emmeline (Emily) GARMAN) was born on 6 Jun 1845 in German Valley, New Jersey. He died on 10 Mar 1911 in Buda, Bureau Co, Illinois.
Note 1: Cemetery says Weise, Jacob E. gives birth and death, military unit: Co C, 93 Reg Ill Vol.
Note 2: Wise in 1850 census, Weise in 1860!
Note 3: WS#6: Made last Will in Buda, in 1907, 3 Jul. Have copy. Jacob and Minnie both signed as Weise!
Note 4: 1877 Concord Twp, Bureau Co, Voters and Taxpayers list has Jacob E. Weise, Buda,

laborer, Dem, born NJ, one child. 1910 census has Jacob and Minnie, ages 64 and 50, own income, Union Army veteran; married 4 years, Minnie, no children.
Note 5: From Weise Genealogy, per David Weise letter, 19 Mar 1996: "Jacob E. Weise, who was adopted by John Trimmer Weise, who raised him and gave him the name Weise."

Margaret (Maggie) KINNICK and Jacob E. WEISE had the following children:

+54   i. **Harry E. WEISE**, born in Sep 1872, Illinois; married La Adell "Ella" MARTIN, on 24 Dec 1899, Harvey, Illinois; died after 1930.

+55   ii. **Roy E. WEISE**, born on 12 Aug 1881; died on 25 Feb 1946, Harvey, Illinois.

11. **Fanny Susan KINNICK** (Susanna (Susan) SCHWYHART-1) was born on 1 Nov 1851 in Bureau Co, Illinois. She died on 18 Feb 1926 in Ohio Twp, Ness Co, Kansas. She was buried in Utica City Cemetery, Utica, Ness Co, Kansas.
Note 1: 1860 census; 1953 KG book: Sue Kinnick Lyons, m Jean Lyons; no children it says [Error, of course, see below]
Note 2: Fanny S. on marriage certificate
Note 3: Living in Utica, KS, in 1923, per Jacob estate.
Note 4: Birth estimate from marriage application
Note 5: Witnesses to marriage, Jacob Weiss, Maggie Weise.
Note 6: Listed in 1920 census, Ness Co, William E, age 68 and Fanny, age 68, including hired help, Claud Burkhead, age 17 (b. KS).
Note 7: Mazie (Fletcher) Ross comment, rec'd from Violet Lowe, 8-23-96: Of course, I remember Aunt Sue. She married Jean Lyon. They lived in Kansas. That is where the Fletchers got the Kansas land.
Note 8: 23 May 1997, visited Ness Co, located extensive land records, Probate records, burial site of William Eugene and Susan Fanny (Kinnick) Lyon, as well as that they had a seven year old son, who died in 1894, Harry. Susan death date stated in book, Requim, Ness Co Historical Museum, even tho stone says 1851-1925. Birth date, 1 Nov 1851.
Note 9: Obit in Ness County News (located 13 Aug 1997): Mr. and Mrs. Lyon came to Greenwood County in the spring of 1880, coming to Ness county in the spring of 1884, where they have resided ever since.

Fanny Susan KINNICK and William Eugene LYON were married on 30 Dec 1879 in Buda, Bureau Co, Illinois.

William Eugene LYON (son of Nathan LYON and Roxane BATES) was born on 19 May 1851 in Warrensville, Ohio. He died on 17 Aug 1930 in Ohio Twp, Ness Co, Kansas. He was buried in Utica City Cemetery, Utica, Ness Co, Kansas.
Note 1: Signed marriage doc Wm. Eugene Lyons, name on front William E. Lyons; implies he may have gone my Eugene, not William or Bill.
Note 2: Birth place and birth date estimate from marriage documents.
Note 3: William and Fannie both residents of Mineral, IL at time of marriage.
Note 4: 23 May 1997, visited Ness Co, located extensive land records, Probate records, burial site of William Eugene and Susan Fanny (Kinnick) Lyon, as well as that they had a seven year old son, who died in 1894, Harry.

Note 5: Obit obtained 13 Aug 1997: Has birth date and place; settled in Greenwood Co in the fall of 1869. He returned to Illinois and was united in marriage to Miss Fannie Kinnic, December 31, 1879, at Mineral, Illinois, where they lived a short time. He moved with his family to Ness County in 1882, and located on a homestead one and a half miles south of Utica, which has been his home since.... Mr. Lyon suffered a stroke on Jan 8, 1930. He was taken to Wakeeney for medical treatment April 3. On May 4 he was taken to the Midwest hospital in Ransom, where he remained until his death.

Fanny Susan KINNICK and William Eugene LYON had the following children:

56   i.   **Harry LYON** was born on 5 Mar 1887 in Ness Co, Kansas. He died on 15 Sep 1894 in Ohio Twp, Ness Co, Kansas. He was buried in Utica City Cem, Utica, Ness Co, Kansas.
Note 1: 23 May 1997, visited Ness Co, located extensive land records, Probate records, burial site of William Eugene and Susan Fanny (Kinnick) Lyon, as well as that they had a seven year old son, who died in 1894, Harry. Stone says b. 15 Sep 1894, 7 yr, 6 mo, 10 d. Calculated 5 Mar 1887 birth.
Note In 1985, the Utica Cemetery Board erected a special stone, next to his parents, in recognition that he was the first person to be place in the Utica Cemetery. It is a very special stone.

Third Generation

12. **Eveline HARRISON** (Mary E. KINNICK-2, Susanna (Susan) SCHWYHART-1) was born on 21 Dec 1854 in Wyanet, Bureau Co, Illinois. She died on 2 Jan 1934 in at home, Estherville, Emmet Co, Iowa. She was buried in Oak Hill Cemetery, Estherville, Emmet Co, Iowa.
Note 1: Alive in 1923.
Note 2: 2-26-96: Got packet from Emmet Co with info on three gen of her family name listed as Evaline.
Note 3: 1870 census has Eveline, age 15, with Susan, grandmother.
Note 4: 15 Mar 96 ltr, see Francis, says they also had a son who died in infancy.
Note 5: Per 1925 census data, Evaline in Iowa 30 years, came in 1895.
Note 6: Details added from Lush book via Walter G. Elwell 4/3/96; has more bio.

Eveline HARRISON and Francis (Frank) HORNBY were married on 22 Jan 1876 in Illinois.

Francis (Frank) HORNBY was born on 21 Jan 1847 in Big Rock, Kane Co, Illinois. He died on 18 Jan 1915. He was buried in Oak Hill Cemetery, Estherville, Emmet Co, Iowa.
Note 1: Frank and Eveline Hornby purchased the NE 1/4 of Section 18, Township 99 North of Range 33, Emmet Co, Iowa, on September 10, 1890. They came from Sheffield, IL. They had a family of eight children....They were members of the Methodist Church and are buried at Oak Hill Cemetery. ...from Emmet Co History, Vol III. Ltr 15 Mar 1996 from Jeanne Egeland, Emmet Co: Fancis, Eveline, Richard and Burton buried at Oak Hill in Block 8 lot 75, spaces 1, 2, 3, & 4. "When a small boy he came with his parents to their homestead three miles northeast of

Sheffield, IL. Here he grew to manhood and then cared for his aged parents. He enlisted in the 64th IL volunteers and served a year and a half during the Civil war." Details added from Lush book via Walter G. Elwell 4/3/96; has more bio.

Eveline HARRISON and Francis (Frank) HORNBY had the following children:

+57   i.   **Harry E. HORNBY**, born on 12 Feb 1877, Anita, Cass Co, Iowa; married Ida HASBROOK, on 12 Dec 1900, Princeton, Bureau Co, Illinois; died on 2 Dec 1953.

+58   ii.   **Blanche Frances HORNBY**, born on 16 Feb 1879, Anita, Cass Co, Iowa; died on 11 Dec 1970, Los Angeles, California.

+59   iii.   **Richard George HORNBY**, born on 28 Dec 1880, Bureau Co, Illinois; married Sophia HARMS, in 1911, White, South Dakota.

+60   iv.   **Mabel Gertrude HORNBY**, born on 21 Apr 1883, Concord Twp, Bureau Co, Illinois; married Henry A. WAGNER, on 22 Jun 1906; died on 12 Oct 1914, Laramie Co, Wyoming.

+61   v.   **Glennie May HORNBY**, born on 17 Oct 1885, Concord Twp, Bureau Co, Illinois; married Guy Carlton STEARNS, on 16 Nov 1904; died on 29 Jan 1934, Grand Meadows, Minnesota.

62   vi.   **Ralph HORNBY** was born on 17 Oct 1885. He died on 16 Jan 1888.
Note 1: Details added from Lush book via Walter G. Elwell 4/3/96; a twin of Glennie; death date.

+63   vii.   **Fannie Estella HORNBY**, born on 8 Jun 1888, Concord Twp, Bureau Co, Illinois; married Charles Henry (Charley) SLININGER, on 4 Sep 1907, Estherville, Emmet Co, Iowa; died on 15 May 1973.

+64   viii.   **Mina Irene HORNBY**, born on 16 Oct 1891, Concord Twp, Bureau Co, Illinois; married Stanley Boyd HIGLEY, in Dec 1910, Estherville, Emmet Co, Iowa; died on 17 Apr 1926.

65   ix.   **Burton HORNBY** was born on 31 Mar 1896 in Concord Twp, Bureau Co, Illinois. He died on 16 Aug 1937 in Estherville, Emmet Co, Iowa. He was buried in Oak Hill Cemetery, Estherville, Emmet Co, Iowa.
Note 1: Per 1920 census, says cannot speak English, cannot read or write.
Note 2: Alive when mother Eveline died 1 Jan 1934, living in Estherville.
Note 3: Died in 1937 per Oak Hill records. Details added from Lush book via Walter G. Elwell 4/3/96; birth and death date specifics

14. **Almira RICHMOND** (Sarah Ann KINNICK-2, Susanna (Susan) SCHWYHART-1) was born about 1855. She died about 1918. She was buried in Forest Hill Cemetery, Wyanet, Bureau Co, Illinois.
Note 1: Died before 1923, per Jacob estate (question session in error, here).
Note 2: Per Jet Hall 27 Nov 95 Info, birth and death dates, has Almyra (sp?)
Note 3: 1870 census, Almira, age 15, says born in Missouri!!
Note 4: Delos remarried by 1 Dec 1892.

Almira RICHMOND and Delos LAY were married in 1877.

Delos LAY was born about 1858 in Wisconsin. He died on 25 Mar 1935 in Concord Twp,

Bureau Co, IL.

Note 1: Per Jet Hall 27 Nov 95 Info, first name 1920 Census for daughter, Olive, says Delos born in WI 1910 census has second wife and two children, born in WI; Boarder, Blanch E. Sargent, born NE, age 18

Note 2: 1900 census, Wyanet, Bureau Co, IL, has: Delos M. Lay household, 1900 U. S. Census, Wyanet Township, Bureau County, Illinois, page , dwelling 262, family 265, has Delos, born March 1857, age 43, married 23 years, born in Michigan, Farmer, with wife, Almira, born December 1854, age 45, married 23 years, four children, all living and listed, born Illinois. Children: Charles D., son, born September 1878, age 21, single, born in Illinois, Farm Laborer; Henry C., son, born December 1880, 19, single, born in Illinois; Olive M., daughter, born June 1883, age 16, single, born in Illinois, At School; and Helen E., daughter, born September 1885, age 14, single, born in Illinois, At School; with "servant" Redenius Mienert, born September 1879, age 20, single, born in Kansas, Farm Laborer (he married Olive, about a year after this census report).

Almira RICHMOND and Delos LAY had the following children:

+66	i.	**Charles D. LAY**, born in Sep 1878, Illinois.
+67	ii.	**Clare H. LAY**, born on 26 Dec 1880, Illinois; died on 12 Jul 1965, Butte Co, CA.
+68	iii.	**Olive May (Ollie) LAY**, born in Jun 1883, Illinois; died before 1984.
+69	iv.	**Helen LAY**, born in Sep 1885, Illinois; died before 1923.

16. **Sarah RICHMOND** (Sarah Ann KINNICK-2, Susanna (Susan) SCHWYHART-1) was born in Oct 1860 in Missouri.

Note 1: Sarah A. Hackett Household. 1900 U. S. Census, population schedule, Illinois, Bureau County, Fairfield Township, p. 5B, dwelling 89, family 92. Sarah A. Hackett, Head, born Oct 1860, age 39, Widowed, six children, five living, born in Missouri, father born in Iowa, mother born in Ohio, occupation: Farmer. Also in the household are four daughters, a niece and a servant. Daughter, Laura A., born October 1883, age 16, single, born in Illinois, (for all four daughters) father born in New Jersey, mother born in Missouri. Daughter, Fannie J., was born February 1886, age 14, born in Illinois, at school. Daughter, Grace B., was born November 1889, age 10, single, born in Illinois, at school. Daughter, Bessie E., was born October 1891, single, born in Illinois. Niece, Stella Dingman, born in June 1896, age 3, single, born in New Mexico, father born in Nebraska, mother born in Illinois. Servant, George Sinning, male, born in August 1878, age 26, single, he and both parents born in Germany, not a citizen, Farm laborer, does read, write and speak English.

Note 2: She died on 13 Mar 1935.

Note 3: Living in Tampico, IL, in 1923, per Jacob estate. [Whitehead County!]

Note 4: Per Jet Hall 27 Nov 95 Info, birth and death date, her middle name, his first name.

Note 5: 1910 census has her in Bureau Co, Fairfield Twp, with daughter. Bessie, age 18, and Niece, Stella Dingman; says father born in Iowa.

Note 6: 1870 census has Sarah, age 9. Not with mother in 1880.

Note 7: Sarah A. Hackett Household. 1900 U. S. Census, population schedule, Illinois, Bureau County, Fairfield Township, p. 5B, dwelling 89, family 92. Sarah A. Hackett, Head, born Oct 1860, age 39, Widowed, six children, five living, born in Missouri, father born in Iowa, mother born in Ohio, occupation: Farmer. Also in the household are four daughters, a niece and a servant. Daughter, Laura A., born October 1883, age 16, single, born in Illinois, (for all four daughters) father born in New Jersey, mother born in Missouri. Daughter, Fannie J., was born February 1886, age 14, born in Illinois, at school. Daughter, Grace B., was born November 1889, age 10, single, born in Illinois, at school. Daughter, Bessie E., was born October 1891, single, born in Illinois. Niece, Stella Dingman, born in June 1896, age 3, single, born in New Mexico, father born in Nebraska, mother born in Illinois. Servant, George Sinning, male, born in August 1878, age 26, single, he and both parents born in Germany, not a citizen, Farm laborer, does read, write and speak English.

Note 8: Illinois Statewide Death Index, 1916-1950: Sarah Ann Hackett, female, white, age 74, Cert# 12795, 13 March 1935, Whiteside County, City: Tampico.

John HACKETT was born in 1848 in New Jersey. He died before 1900.
Note 1: Per Jet Hall 27 Nov 95 Info, his first name
Note 2: Born in New Jersey, per daughter, Bessie 1910 census data.
Note 3: Died before 1900, see wife's census.
Note 4: John Hackett Household. 1880 U. S. Census, population schedule, Illinois, Bureau County, Fairfield Township, p. 5B, dwelling 164, family 167. John Hackett, Head, male, age 32, Farmer, born in New Jersey, both parents born in New Jersey, his wife, Sarah, age 21, Keeping house, born in Missouri, father born in U. S., mother born in Ohio. Daughter, Eva, age 8, born in Illinois, father born in New Jersey, mother born in Missouri; daughter, Iniss, age 8/12, born in October, in Illinois, father born in New Jersey, mother born in Missouri.

Sarah RICHMOND and John HACKETT had the following children:

70	i.	**Eva HACKETT** was born in 1872 in Illinois.
		Note 1: See father's 1880 census
71	ii.	**Iniss HACKETT** was born in Oct 1879 in Illinois.
		Note 1: See father's 1880 census
72	iii.	**Laura A. HACKETT** was born in Oct 1883 in Illinois.
		Note 1: From mother's 1900 census report
73	iv.	**Fannie J. HACKETT** was born in Feb 1886 in Illinois.
		Note 1: From mother's 1900 census
74	v.	**Grace B. HACKETT** was born in Nov 1889 in Illinois.
		Note 1: From mother's 1900 census
75	vi.	**Bessie HACKETT** was born in Oct 1891 in Illinois.
		Note 1: See mother's 1900 census

17. **Laura A. RICHMOND** (Sarah Ann KINNICK-2, Susanna (Susan) SCHWYHART-1) was born on 24 Jul 1862 in Bureau Co, Illinois. She died on 11 Jul 1905 in Allison, Butler Co, IA. She was buried in Lynwood Cemetery, Clarksville, Butler Co, IA.
Note 1: Died before 1923, per Jacob estate.
Note 2: Per Jet Hall 27 Nov 95 Info, middle name, birth and death date
Note 3: p. 25, 1880 census, has France and Laura in household 44! Age 21 & 17.
Note 4: 1870 census has Laura, age 8, with parents.
Note 5: Death Cert. from Leonard and Crystal Hanson has birth and death dates and middle initial.

Note 6: Her Obit says she married 3 Sep 1879 and they moved in the fall of 1884 to Butler Co, IA. They had lived for the past 16 years on the M.J. Perrin farm near Allison, where she passed away. She died after 'a long suffering with cancer.'

Laura A. RICHMOND and Francis Newton (F. N.) SCOTT were married on 3 Sep 1879 in Bureau Co, Illinois.

Francis Newton (F. N.) SCOTT was born about 1859. He died about 20 Feb 1941 in Allison, Butler Co, IA. He was buried in Lynwood Cemetery, Clarksville, Butler Co, IA.
Note 1: Per Jet Hall 27 Nov 95 Info, first and middle name (France Noton).
Note 2: Correct name from death notice in newspaper in Clarksville, IA, library.
Note 3: Death date shown in date of newspaper. Said he died 'Monday afternoon' and came to Butler Co, IA, from Illinois about sixty years ago. For many years he lived on a farm southeast of Allison, later retiring to that town. For a number of years he had been caretaker of the Allison cemetery. Mentions his widow (not named), the lists the children 'from a previous marriage.'

Laura A. RICHMOND and Francis Newton (F. N.) SCOTT had the following children:

+76	i.	**William Henry SCOTT**, born on 4 Nov 1881, Princeton, Bureau Co, IL; married Myra BANDFIELD, on 30 Jun 1909; married Lillie Hilke FREESE, on 23 Jun 1920, Waverly, IA; died on 15 May 1931, Allison, Butler Co, IA.
+77	ii.	**Claude SCOTT**, born in Oct 1883, Illinois; died on 6 Feb 1962.
+78	iii.	**Jessie SCOTT**, born on 26 Oct 1883; died before 1895.
+79	iv.	**Olive "Ollie" SCOTT**, born on 19 Jul 1885, Allison, Butler Co, Iowa; died on 29 Jul 1979, Mason City, Cerro Gordo Co, IA.
+80	v.	**Ray SCOTT**, born on 7 Jan 1892; married Nellie WILSEY, on 20 Aug 1912; died on 11 Aug 1964.
81	vi.	**Emery SCOTT** was born on 13 Jul 1894. He died on 19 Jan 1963. Note 1: Living in Allison, IA, in 1923. Note 2: Father's obit says: 'of Allison' in Feb 1941.
+82	vii.	**Eugene SCOTT**, born in 1895.
+83	viii.	**Sheldon SCOTT**, born on 4 Sep 1897, near Allison, Butler Co, IA; married Hester Hazel WEST, on 24 May 1915; died on 15 Jan 1958, Iowa City, Johnson Co, IA.
84	ix.	**Louise SCOTT** was born in 1899 in Butler County, Iowa.
+85	x.	**John SCOTT**, born in 1900; died on 8 Dec 1925.
+86	xi.	**Josie SCOTT**, born in 1901; died after 1941.
87	xii.	**Jennie SCOTT** was born about 1903. Born before 1905; she died before 1905.
88	xiii.	**Lillian SCOTT** was born about 1904. Born before 1905; she died before 1905.

18. **Frances Belle (Belle) RICHMOND** (Sarah Ann KINNICK-2, Susanna (Susan) SCHWYHART-1) was born about 1865. She died about 1895.
Note 1: Died before 1923 per Jacob estate.
Note 2: Per Jet Hall 27 Nov 95 Info, birth and death date, name Frances Bell
Note 3: 1870 census has Bell T., age 4, with parents; 1880 census has Bell, age 14, with mother.

Frances Belle (Belle) RICHMOND and George DINGMAN married.

George DINGMAN – not more information available.
Note 1: Per Jet Hall 27 Nov 95 Info, first name

Frances Belle (Belle) RICHMOND and George DINGMAN had the following children:

+89   i.   **Myra D. DINGMAN**, born in Jan 1894, Nebraska.
+90   ii.   **Estella "Stella" DINGMAN**, born in Jun 1896, New Mexico.

19.   **John W. RICHMOND** (Sarah Ann KINNICK-2, Susanna (Susan) SCHWYHART-1) was born in Nov 1867 in Illinois. He died about 1939. He was buried in Forest Hill Cemetery, Wyanet, Bureau Co, Illinois.
Note 1: Lived in Wyanet, IL, in 1923, per Jacob estate.
Note 2: Per Jet Hall 27 Nov 95 Info, birth and death dates
Note 3: Listed in 1920 Soundex in rural Bureau Co, age 52.
Note 4: 1900 Soundex has John W. at age 32, Bureau Co, Wyanet Twp., includes Lydia, Leroy, Everett and Rose Hall, Lydia's sister, age 28. Rose married Ora Fletcher later in the year 1900!
Note 5: 1870 census says age 2, 1880 census says age 12.
Note 6: 1910 census, age 43 with family. Also, Rose D Ammon, age 17, as servant.
Note 7: 1920 census, Concord Twp, Bureau Co, IL, has: John W. Richmond, 52, IL, US, OH, Threshing; with wife, Lydia, 52, IL, OH, IL; with son, LeRoy, 25 (all children born in IL), son, Evert, 20, Russell, 18, Howard, 15, dau Mae, 15, Son Vivars, 9.
Note 8: 1930 census, Wyanet Village, Wyanet Twp, Bureau Co, IL, has: John Richmond, 62, M first at 25, IL, Can, VA, Odd jobs; with wife, Lydia, 63, IL, OH, IL, and son, Everett, 31, S, IL3.
Note 9: John W. Richmond household, 1900 U. S. Census, household schedule, Illinois, Bureau County, Wyanet Township, 27 Jun 1900: John W. Richmond, Head, born Nov 1867, age 32, married 7 years, born Illinois, father and mother both born in Ohio, Farm Laborer; Wife, Lydia, A, born Feb 1867, age 33, married 7 years, three children, two living and listed, born in Illinois, father born in Ohio, mother born in Illinois; Son, Leroy D., born Aug 1894, age 5, single, self, father and mother born in Illinois; Son Everett A., born Feb 1899, age 1, single, self, father and mother born in Illinois.

John W. RICHMOND and Lydia Ann II HALL were married about 1892.

Lydia Ann II HALL (daughter of Justus (Jet) HALL and Mary MCNEIL) was born in Feb 1867 in Illinois. She died about 1943. She was buried in Forest Hill Cemetery, Wyanet, Bureau Co, Illinois.
Note 1: Per Jet Hall 27 Nov 95 Info, existence and family
Note 2: Listed on 1920 Soundex, age 52.
Note 3: 1900 census says age 33, born Feb 1861

John W. RICHMOND and Lydia Ann II HALL had the following children:

+91   i.   **Leroy D. RICHMOND**, born in Aug 1894, Illinois; married Halsey A. HALL, in 1921, Illinois; died about 1980.
92   ii.   **Jessie RICHMOND** was born about 1896. She died about 1898.

93	iii.	**Everett C. RICHMOND** was born on 18 Feb 1899 in Illinois. He died on 15 Aug 1967 in Bureau Co, Illinois. He was buried in Forest Hill Cemetery, Wyanet, Bureau Co, Illinois.

Note 1: Per Jet Hall 27 Nov 95 Info

Everett C. RICHMOND was born on 18 Feb 1899 in Illinois. He died on 15 Aug 1967 in Bureau Co, Illinois. He was buried in Forest Hill Cemetery, Wyanet, Bureau Co, Illinois.

Note 1: Per Jet Hall 27 Nov 95 Info

Note 2: 20 on 1920 Soundex.

Note 3: 1900 census says Everett A. born Feb 1899

Note 4: 1910 census says Everett C., I copied, age not copied!

Note 5: 1920 and 1930 with parents.

Note 6: Cemetery inscription says died 1968

Note 7: SSDI has Everett C. Richmond, b. 18 Feb 1899, d. 15 Aug 1967, issued IL, last res: 61356, Princeton, Bureau Co, IL.

+94 iv. **Russell J. RICHMOND**, born about 1901, Illinois; married Blanche M. DAILEY, in 1926; died about 1976.

+95 v. **Howard (twin) RICHMOND**, born about 1904, Illinois; married Mabel Darlene MEEK, in 1928, Illinois; died about 1987.

+96 vi. **Rose Mae (twin) RICHMOND**, born about 1904, Illinois; married Floyd (Pete) WYATT, in 1921; died about 1984.

+97 vii. **Vivian RICHMOND**, born about 1910, Illinois; died about 1985.

20. **Aron I. RICHMOND** (Sarah Ann KINNICK-2, Susanna (Susan) SCHWYHART-1) was born in Dec 1869. He died after 1923.

Note 1: Living in 1923 in Milan, WI, per Jacob estate.

Note 2: Per Jet Hall 27 Nov 95 Info middle initial, birth date, and family

Note 3: 1900 census, has Aron I. in Bureau Co., Concord Twp., renting a farm, with family, including mother, Sarah, and niece, Myra Dingman. Says father born in Canada!!

Note 4: 1870 has Aaron I. age 6/12, 1880 census has Aaron, age 10.

Note 5: Aron I. Richmond household, 1900 U.S. census, population schedule, Illinois, Bureau County, Concord township, p. 4A, dwelling 59, family 59, has Aron I. Richmond, born December 1869, age 30, married for 10 years, born Illinois, father born in Canada, mother born in Ohio, Farmer; with wife, Eva M., born in April 1872, age 28, married 10 years, four children, all alive and listed, born in Illinois, father born in New Jersey, mother born in Illinois. Children (each single, born in Illinois, both parents born in Illinois): Son, John F., born May 1891, age 9; son, William, born in February 1893, age 7; daughter, Jennie M., born June 1896, age 3; daughter, Olive, born in November 1898, age 1. Also in the household, his mother, Sarah A., born in April 1836, age 64, divorced, two children, both alive, born in Ohio, father born in Maryland, mother born in Pennsylvania; as well as Myra D. Dingman, niece, born in January 1894, age 6, single, born in Nebraska, father and mother both born in Illinois.

Aron I. RICHMOND and Evelyne May HACKETT married – details not available.

Evelyne May HACKETT was born in Apr 1872 in Illinois.

Note 1: Per Jet Hall 27 Nov 95 Info

Note 2: 1900 census has birth month and year.

Aron I. RICHMOND and Evelyne May HACKETT had the following children:

98	i.	**John F. RICHMOND** was born in May 1891 in Illinois.

John F. RICHMOND was born in May 1891 in Illinois.
Note 1: Per Jet Hall 27 Nov 95 Info, has name spelled Johnn
Note 2: 1900 census says John F. born May 1891

99   ii. **Wm. RICHMOND** was born in Feb 1893 in Illinois.
Note 1: Per Jet Hall 27 Nov 95 Info
Note 2: 1900 Census says William, born Feb 1893.

100   iii. **Jennie M. RICHMOND** was born in Jun 1896 in Illinois.
Note 1: Per Jet Hall 27 Nov 95 Info
Note 2: 1900 census says Jennie M. born Jun 1896

101   iv. **Olive RICHMOND** was born in Nov 1898 in Illinois.
Note 1: Per Jet Hall 27 Nov 95 Info
Note 2: 1900 census says Olive born Nov 1898

23. Margaret Susana (Maggie) KINNICK (Joseph-2, Susanna (Susan) SCHWYHART-1) was born on 5 Jan 1863 in Bureau Co, Illinois. She died on 23 Aug 1951 in Mill Creek, Park County, Montana.
Note 1: Marriage record found in Greenfield Library, 10-7-95
Note 2: Living in Fry, Montana, in 1923, per Jacob estate.
Note 3: From Marcella Mickel: Rock Island, 14 March 1865: "a little daughter of Mrs. KINNICK, living about 6 miles above Sheffield in Bureau County, died in a fire last Thursday aged about 5 y. She was alone in the home at the time with another child, aged 18m. Mr. Kinnick is a soldier." This appears to be Amanda who died, the younger sister is Margaret. Joseph was mustered out of the Civil War service in St. Louis on 10 March 1865.
Note 4: 1900 census for son, Mark Edick, age 12, with father, William H., says divorced, living with his mother, Rachel A. Edick (found her after reading Joseph Kinnick pension file).
Note 5: Death year and place per Rebecca Fraas, email Nov 1999 (had Mill Creek)
Note 6: Death date and county, per Montana Death Index, 1907-2002, ancestry.com

Margaret Susana (Maggie) KINNICK and William H. (Bill) EDICK were married on 13 Apr 1882 in Greenfield, Adair Co, Iowa.

William H. (Bill) EDICK (son of Alonzo P. (Lon) EDICK and Rachel Ann SCHWYHART) was born in Jan 1856 in Illinois. He died on 28 Jan 1934 in Mill Creek, Park County, Montana.
Note 1: Marriage record found in Greenfield, IA, Library, 10-7-95 (Nancy)
Note 2: 1900 census, Park Co, MT, divorced, age 44, living with his mother and son, Mark, age 12; born Jan 1856, IL, father b. NY, mother b. OH. Engineer (Station, I believe it says).
Note 3: Death year and place Per Rebecca Fraas, email Nov 1999. Also: (Bill and Maggie) moved to Mill Creek, Park County, MT, in 1889 following Lon and Rachel Ann Edick's move to Mill Creek in 1885. Mark is Lon and Rachel Ann's Grandson. Mark has a brother Verner, and a sister Nellie.
Note 4: They are 2nd cousins!
Note 5: Montana Death Index, 1907-2002, has William H Edick, Death date: 28 Jan 1934

Margaret Susana (Maggie) KINNICK and William H. (Bill) EDICK had the following children:

+102   i. **Helen EDICK**, born in Aug 1882, Iowa; married Jesse W. NELSON, in 1905.

103	ii.	**Clarence J. EDICK** was born in Nov 1884 in Iowa. (Helen Edick search) Note 1: 1900 census, Wyoming, Big Horn County, Cody, p. 13B, dwelling 304, family 309 has Margaret Edick, Jan 1863, 37, D, 3,3, IL, OH, OH, Hotel Keeper, with daughter, Helen E. Aug 1882, 17, S, IA, IL, IL, At School, Son, Clarence J., Nov 1884, 15, S, same, Son, Mark, Jan 1888, 12, S, Montana, IL, IL, At School
+104	iii.	**Mark EDICK**, born on 14 Jan 1886, Clyde Park, Park Co, Montana; died on 23 Jun 1970, Chehalis Hosp, Chehalis, Lewis Co, Washington.

24. **William Walter KINNICK** (Joseph-2, Susanna (Susan) SCHWYHART-1) was born on 15 Mar 1866 in Bureau Co, Illinois. He died on 17 Apr 1946 in Livingston, Montana.
Note 1: Living in Park City, Montana, in 1923, per Jacob estate.
Note 2: Listed on birth certificate of 7th child, Dorothea, as Hotel-Keeper, Feb 1919
Note 3: 1900 Federal census - Montana, Yellowstone Co, Park City Precinct: Wm. Kinnick, age 33, b. Mar 1867, married 3 years, b. IL, f.b. IL, m.b. IA. Farmer; with wife, Liliam, age 27, b. Dec 1872 IA, f.b. England, m.b. Scotland. 2 children, 1 living.
Note 4: Death place per daughter, Linda, Aug 1999.
Note 5: 1930 census has William W, 64, IL, and Jo Andalupe, 40, Kinnick, with Myuel A, 20, Rachel A, 18, J William, 15, John P, 12, Dorthy E, 10, Thomas S, 8, Edward M, 6, and Frederick W, 3 10/12, at Upper Mill Creek, Park Co, MT.

William Walter KINNICK and Guadelupe Ramono COVURRUBIAS were married in 1907/8.

Guadelupe Ramono COVURRUBIAS (daughter of Miguel Angel CAVARRUBIAS and Amelia ALVAREZLE) was born on 28 Feb 1890 in Mexico City, Mexico. She died on 17 Apr 1977. She was buried in Park View Memorial Garden, Livingston, Montana.
Note 1: Last name per Dorothea birth certificate; first name misspelled; also, 1920 fed census has her age 29 (1891). Sketch says she was nineteen and William 42 (1908) when married (so, 1889). Died 1976 at age of eighty seven (1889).
Note 2: v instead of b, per letter of 8-12-97 from Mary Kinnick, son Bill's wife; age 24 on William Joseph's birth certificate.
Note 3: Middle name per John P. sheet, from his daughter Linda, Aug 1999; also, full birth and death dates and places and burial place, and parents full names.
Note 4: 1930 census has William W, 64, IL, and Jo Andalupe, 40, Kinnick, with Myuel A, 20, Rachel A, 18, J William, 15, John P, 12, Dorthy E, 10, Thomas S, 8, Edward M, 6, and Frederick W, 3 10/12, at Upper Mill Creek, Park Co, MT.

William Walter KINNICK and Guadelupe Ramono COVURRUBIAS had the following children:

+105	i.	**Miquel Angel (Mike) KINNICK**, born on 13 Aug 1909, Mexico City, Mexico; married Julia SUTHERLAND, on 12 Jul 1939, Lutheran, Livingston, Montana; died on 15 Mar 1972, Park Co, Montana.
+106	ii.	**Rachel Amelia KINNICK**, born on 3 Jan 1911, San Antonio, Texas; married Virgil Clark NICKERSON, on 6 Apr 1935, Livingston, Montana; married Ed OLSON, on 19 May 1997.

+107	iii.	**Guadelupe Margaret (Marge) KINNICK**, born on 24 Sep 1912, San Antonio, Texas.
+108	iv.	**William Joseph (Woody) KINNICK**, born on 16 Jul 1914, San Antonio, Bexar Co, Texas; married Mary Evangeline SNEATH, on 29 Mar 1945, Rocky Ford, Colorado; died on 2 Apr 1996, Marian Med Center, Santa Maria, Santa Barbara Co, California.
109	v.	**Infant KINNICK** was born in 1915 in Texas. He died in 1915 in Texas. Note 1: Per 1920 census Note 2: 24 Jun 1997, received 1984 Park County History sketch of William Walter Kinnick with extensive family detail. This child not included in ten mentioned thru the year; assume died shortly after 1920, if real. Note 3: Died at birth, from Dorothy Adams, 15 Aug 1997.
+110	vi.	**John Porfirio KINNICK**, born on 29 Jan 1917, Park City, Yellowstone Co, Montana; married Earlene Delores LEFFINGWELL, on 16 Nov 1940, Livingston, Montana; died on 29 Mar 1999, Clarkson, Washington.
+111	vii.	**Dorothy Elizabeth KINNICK**, born on 6 Feb 1919, Huntley, Yellowstone Co, Montana; married Joseph Thomas (Joe) ADAMS, on 16 Feb 1947, Livingston, Montana; died on 25 Aug 1997, Park, Montana.
+112	viii.	**Thomas Jesse (Tom) KINNICK**, born on 15 Feb 1921, Hilda, Taney Co, Missouri; married Margie EDWARDS, on 16 Jun 1946, Baptist, Livingston, Montana; died on 20 Jul 1993, Livingston, Park Co, Montana.
+113	ix.	**Edward Mark (Ed) KINNICK**, born on 31 Mar 1924, Livingston, Park County, Montana; died on 15 Apr 1998, Park Co, Montana.
+114	x.	**Fred Walter KINNICK**, born on 12 May 1926, Livingston, Park County, Montana.
+115	xi.	**George Alvin KINNICK**, born on 4 Dec 1930, Livingston, Park County, Montana; married Carolee PARKER, on 25 Apr 1954, Episcopal, Livingston, Park Co, Montana.

William Walter KINNICK second married Lilian UNKNOWN in 1897.

Lilian UNKNOWN was born in Dec 1872 in Iowa.
Note 1: 1900 census (see husband)

25. **John Leach Cook KINNICK** (Joseph-2, Susanna (Susan) SCHWYHART-1) was born on 22 Mar 1868 in near, Buda, Bureau Co, Illinois. He died on 7 May 1935 in Laurel, Stillwater Co, Montana. He was buried in May 1935 in Park City, Stillwater Co, Montana.
Note 1: Living in Laurel, Montana, in 1923, per Jacob estate
Note 2: More details on John Leach Cook Kinnick family from Marcella Mickel, a granddaughter, via Susie Bromley, 2-5-96.
Note 3: 1900 Federal census - Montana, Yellowstone Co, Park City Precinct: John, 32, Lizzie, 29, married 9 years, 4 children, all living: Myrtle, 9, Ernest, 7, John, 4, Jessie, 2; also two farm laborer "helpers."
Note 4: Montana Death Index, 1907-2002 (ancestry.com) has 8 May 1935

John Leach Cook KINNICK and Ida Elizabeth (Lizzie) MCAFERTY were married on 25 Sep 1890 in Billings, Yellowstone Co, Montana.

Ida Elizabeth (Lizzie) MCAFERTY (daughter of James MCAFERTY and Elma Jane WILLCOX) was born on 30 Dec 1870 in near, Winterset, Madison Co, Iowa. She died on 14 Jul 1943 in Laurel, Stillwater Co, Montana. She was buried in Jul 1943 in Park City, Stillwater Co, Montana.
Note 1: Marcella says Ida born "near Winterset, Webster Co, Iowa."

John Leach Cook KINNICK and Ida Elizabeth (Lizzie) MCAFERTY had the following children:

+116	i.	**Myrtle KINNICK**, born on 29 Jul 1891, near, Red Lodge, Carbon Co, Montana; married Joseph Howard LOCHRIDGE, on 5 Dec 1908, Red Lodge, Carbon Co, Montana; died on 17 Jan 1967, nursing home, Spokane, Washington.
117	ii.	**Ernest KINNICK** was born on 27 May 1893 in near, Red Lodge, Carbon Co, Montana. He died on 7 Apr 1908 in Montana. He was buried in Kinnick Family Plot, Park City, Stillwater Co, Montana. Note 1: Per Laurel's Story (1979), from Lyle Jones, 26 Apr 1997: Burial place, age 15.
+118	iii.	**John KINNICK**, born on 1 Oct 1895, near, Red Lodge, Carbon Co, Montana; married Alice Elizabeth MORRELES, on 21 Jan 1922, Missoula, Montana; died on 29 Sep 1969, Klamath Falls, Oregon.
+119	iv.	**Jessie Margaret KINNICK**, born on 24 Nov 1897, near, Red Lodge, Carbon Co, Montana; married William B. ALTIMUS, on 17 Jan 1924; died on 14 Apr 1947, Laurel, Yellowstone Co, Montana.
+120	v.	**Elma Mae (Babe) KINNICK**, born on 1 Feb 1901, Laurel, Yellowstone Co, Montana; married Leo B. MOORE, on 3 May 1910; died on 11 May 1987, PlPines Conv Hospital, Placerville, El Dorado Co, California.
+121	vi.	**Rachel Ann KINNICK**, born on 13 Jul 1906, Laurel, Yellowstone Co, Montana; married Arthur Frederick SCHEIDECKER, on 22 May 1924, Laurel, Yellowstone Co, Montana; married Elmer R. (Dick) GOODENBAUR, about 1937, Laurel, Yellowstone Co, Montana; died on 3 Jun 1983, Seattle, King Co, Washington.

26. **Mary Eppenetes (Mate) KINNICK** (Joseph-2, Susanna (Susan) SCHWYHART-1) was born on 23 May 1870 in Bureau Co, Illinois. She died between 1947 and 1949.
Note 1: Second marriage shown as way to question which was husband.
Note 2: Stoves is question mark? He married "Mate." Is she "Mate"? Who is?
Note 3: Mrs. Mate Stores, living in Cody, WY, in 1923, per Jacob estate.
Note 4: See letter from Rettabelle, dated 2 Nov 1996, say died in 1947, 48, 49.
Note 5: Letter from Rettabelle, received 5 June 1996, says, "I do remember that Aunt Mate married Uncle Luke twice - I can't remember if she married someone else in between - They did have a daughter Margaret." Notice she is saying Luke, not Lute....

"Lute" JONES – more information sought.

Mary Eppenetes (Mate) KINNICK and Martin Luther "Lute" JONES had the following children:
Note 1: XXX means added after report first run

XXX	i.	**Chester W. JONES** was born in Dec 1889 in Wyoming.

XXX   i.   **Chester W. JONES** was born in Dec 1889 in Wyoming.
Note 1: Richard Thayer, Dec 2008 email
Note 2: 1910 U. S. Census

XXX   ii.   **Mabel L. JONES**, born in Jul 1892, Montana; married J. Jones BALLARD.
Note 1: Richard Thayer, Dec 2008 email
Note 2: 1910 U. S. Census

XXX   iii.   **Rachel Ann JONES**, born in June 1897, Wyoming; married Frank KINNE
Note 1: Richard Thayer, Dec 2008 email
Note 2: 1910, 1920, 1930 U. S. Census

XXX   iv.   **Frances J. JONES**, born on 9 Apr 1900, Montana; married Henry Clark PURVIS, in 1918; died 2000, Cody, Wyoming.
Note 1: Richard Thayer, Dec 2008 email
Note 2: 1910, 1930 U.S. Census

XXX   v.   **James A. JONES** was born in 1905 in Wyoming.
Note 1: Richard Thayer, Dec 2008 email
Note 2: 1910 U. S. Census

122   vi.   **Margaretta L. JONES** was born in 1907, in Wyoming; married Samuel Stevenson BRADFORD, in 1930.
Note 1: Per letter from Rettabelle, 5 Jun 1997.
Note 2: Richard Thayer, Dec 2008 email
Note 3: 1910, 1930 U. S. Census

29. George Butler KINNICK (Joseph-2, Susanna (Susan) SCHWYHART-1) was born on 2 Aug 1878 in Adair Co, Iowa. He died on 27 Oct 1972 in Fort Lauderdale, Broward Co, Florida. He was buried on 30 Oct 1972 in Lauderdale Gardens, Fort Lauderdale, Broward Co, Florida.
Note 1: Living in Park City, Montana, in 1923, per Jacob estate
Note 2: Obtained Obit from Broward Co, FL, 5 Aug 1996.
Note 3: 1900 Federal census - Montana, Yellowstone Co, Park City Precinct: George Kinnick, with parents; listed as Sheep Shearer.
Note 4: Confirmed by SSDI, also.
Note 5: 1910 census, School District 24, Yellowstone Co, MT, has: George B. Kinnick, 31, M1 5, IA, IL, WVa, with wife, Belle, 31, M1 5, 1 1, IA OH, WI; with daughter, Ruth E, 4, MT, IA2; and six boarders.
Note 6: 1930 census, 802 14th Terrace S. W., Fort Lauderdale, Broward Co, FL, has: George, 51, first marr at 26, IA3, Farmer, Truck Farm; with wife, Belle, 51 first marr at 26, IA, OH, WI, with dau, Retta Belle, 13, FL, IA2.

George Butler KINNICK and Belle Winnie HOLMES were married in 1905.

Belle Winnie HOLMES was born on 4 Aug 1878 in Iowa. She died on 10 Nov 1955 in Fort Lauderdale, Broward Co, Florida. She was buried on 11 Nov 1955 in Fort Lauderdale, Broward Co, Florida.
Note 1: Per Rettabelle Kinnick Cookus letter, 12 Oct 1996; birth and death info, and maiden and middle name.

George Butler KINNICK and Belle Winnie HOLMES had the following children:

| +123 | i. | **Ruth KINNICK**, born on 27 Dec 1905, Billings, Montana; married James P. SHULL, on 15 Jun 1926, Davie, Florida; died on 6 Jun 1995, Statesville, North Carolina. |
| +124 | ii. | **Rettabelle KINNICK**, born on 4 Mar 1917, Davie, Florida; married Harrison Shull COOKUS, on 12 Nov 1941, Lawton, Oklahoma; died on 7 May 2000, Ft. Lauderdale, Florida. |

32. **Emma Estella KINNICK** (Walter Watson-2, Susanna (Susan) SCHWYHART-1) was born on 9 Dec 1866 in Buda, Bureau Co, Illinois. She died on 4 Mar 1935.
Note 1: Living in Buda, IL, in 1923, per Jacob estate.

Emma Estella KINNICK and William S. (Will) CARPER were married in Jan 1894 in Buda, Bureau Co, Illinois.

William S. (Will) CARPER (son of Jacob S. CARPER and Catherine HORTON) was born about 1867. He died on 13 Feb 1955 in Buda, Bureau Co, Illinois. He was buried in Hopeland Cemetery, Buda, Bureau Co, Illinois.
Note 1: 1930 census has William S. Carper in District 31, Macon Township, Bureau Co, IL, 62, first married at 26, IL, PA, PA, Farmer, Gen Farming, Owns, with wife, Emma E, 63, first married at 27, IL, OH, IL, and nephew, George R. Horton, 11, S, IL, IL, IL.
Note 2: Personal note from Russell & Carolyn (her voice) Stroud, Buda, dated April 18, 1996: "Will Carper and his wife raised Margaret's youngest brother, George Horton, and he is deceased. They lived on a farm SW of Buda." She had noted earlier in the note that she "went to school with Margaret Horton Downer and graduated from Buda Twp. High School in 1932."

33. **Margaret Ann (Maggie) KINNICK** (Walter Watson-2, Susanna (Susan) SCHWYHART-1) was born on 7 Dec 1868 in Buda, Bureau Co, Illinois. She died on 10 Feb 1920 in Buda, Bureau Co, Illinois. She was buried in Hopeland Cemetery, Buda, Bureau Co, Illinois.
Note 1: No children mentioned in "Buda" writeup of Lee Brewer.
Note 2: From Brewer family info: Obit: She was known as Maggie. She was a faithful member of the W.R.C., the D. of R., and R. N. of A. She is survived by her husband and four brothers and four sisters.
Note 3: 1910 census has Lee and Margaret A, ages 47 and 41, married 19 years, no children born nor alive; Walter W. living with them.

Margaret Ann (Maggie) KINNICK and Lee BREWER were married in Jan 1891 in Buda, Bureau Co, Illinois.

Lee BREWER (son of Stephen BREWER and Sarah Augusta ELLIS) was born on 23 Apr 1862 in Muscatine, Iowa. He died on 12 Jan 1946 in East Moline, Illinois. He was buried on 15 Jan 1946 in Hopeland Cemetery, Buda, Bureau Co, Illinois.
Note 1: "Buda" book, p 223, says: He came to Buda when he was 15 years of age and has lived here since. He married Maggie Kinnick, January 1891 and she died in February 1920. He married Ellen Dillman, November 15, 1921 and she died in 1936. He had worked in the railroad shops - followed the carpenter trade and later had a shoe and harness repair shop. He belonged to

the I.O.O.F. lodge for 55 years. He was buried in Hopeland Cemetery. No mention of any children from either marriage.

Note 2: See also, in Bureau Co Report # 4, "Fifth Generation" on Brewer family. It says he was born in Rock Island, IL!

Note 3: Listed in 1910 census as Baggageman for the Railroad.

Note 4: Personal note from Russell & Carolyn (her voice) Stroud, Buda, dated April 18, 1996: "I remember Lee Brewer as he ran a Shoe Repair Shop and Candy Store here in Buda when I was a kid."

34. **Alonzo Palmer KINNICK** (Walter Watson-2, Susanna (Susan) SCHWYHART-1) was born on 2 Nov 1870 in Stuart, Adair Co, Iowa. He died on 27 Feb 1923 in Coon Rapids, Carroll Co, Iowa. He was buried in C. R. Cemetery, Coon Rapids, Carroll Co, Iowa.

Note 1: Alonzo P. Kinnick Household, 1900 U. S. Census, population schedule, Iowa, Carroll County, Union Township, Coon Rapids (Incorporated), dwelling 93, family 93, p. 5A. Alonzo P. Kinnick, Head, born November 1871, age 28, married 8 years, born in Iowa, parents both born in Illinois, occupation: Mason, months not employed, 3, owns his home, free of mortgage. Wife, Margaret N. Kinnick, born September 1869, age 30, married 8 years, three children, three living, born in Iowa, father born in Wales, mother born in Illinois, occupation is blank. Three children listed: Son, Paul H. Kinnick, born August 1892, age 7, single, born in Iowa, both parents born in Iowa, at school; Daughter, Helen L. Kinnick, born March 1894, age 6, single, born in Iowa, both parents born in Iowa, at school; Son, Robert H. Kinnick, born March 1896, age 4, single, born in Iowa, both parents born in Iowa. Also in household, brother, Erastus Kinnick, born November 1865, age 34, single, born in Iowa, parents both born in Illinois, occupation: Farm hand

Note 2: 1895 Iowa Census, Carroll County, A P Kinnick Household: A P Kinnick, 29, Mahaska County, Iowa, Laborer, all family as Protestant; M E Kinnick, 28, Guthrie County; P H Kinnick, 2, Carroll County; H Kinnick, 11 mos, Carroll County; also in household, Geo Kinnick, 22, Missouri, Laborer.

Note 3: From Greenfield Library, Greenfield, IA (10-7-95) Methodist Church Membership list: "A. P. Kinnick, 2 1/2 mi, N.W. Grove Center, 8/9/08, with Mrs. Nettie, and Lucile."

Alonzo Palmer KINNICK and Margaret Jeanette (Nettie) WILLIAMS were married on 6 Jul 1891 in Carroll, Carroll Co, Iowa.

Margaret Jeanette (Nettie) WILLIAMS (daughter of Elias WILLIAMS and Ann Eliza DUNCAN) was born on 20 Sep 1869. She died on 24 Jun 1936. She was buried in C. R. Cemetery, Coon Rapids, Carroll Co, Iowa.

Alonzo Palmer KINNICK and Margaret Jeanette (Nettie) WILLIAMS had the following children:

+125	i.	**Paul Harold KINNICK**, born on 18 Aug 1892; married Dorothy Christine SORENSEN, on 12 Aug 1914, Greenfield, Adair Co, Iowa; died on 1 Apr 1968, Coon Rapids, Carroll Co, Iowa.
+126	ii.	**Helen Lucile KINNICK**, born on 28 Mar 1894, Iowa; married Wilson Cleveland HERRON, on 18 Sep 1912; died on 13 Mar 1956.
+127	iii.	**Robert Haydn KINNICK**, born on 25 Mar 1896; married Edna Pearl

PIERCE, on 2 Dec 1914; died on 9 Nov 1953.

+128   iv.   **Mary Gertrude KINNICK**, born on 1 Oct 1902, Carroll Co, Iowa; married Everett Lyman BRIDESON, on 20 Dec 1921, Kinnick Farm, Coon Rapids, Carroll Co, Iowa; died on 25 Sep 1988, at residence, San Luis Obisbo, California.

+129   v.   **Lillian Roberta KINNICK**, born on 1 May 1908, at home, Greenfield, Adair Co, Iowa; married Delbert Hugh FORD, on 22 Aug 1926, Brideson Farm, Bayard, Guthrie Co, Iowa; died on 17 Aug 1993, Coon Rapids, Iowa.

36. **Ira Odell KINNICK** (Walter Watson-2, Susanna (Susan) SCHWYHART-1) was born on 20 Jul 1874 in Buda, Bureau Co, Illinois. 5 years old in 1880 census, with family.

Note 1: Living in Cheyenne, WY, 2511 Evans St., in 1923, per Jacob estate.

Note 2: Ira O. Kinnick, 1910 U. S. Census, population schedule, South Dakota, 3-Wd Tyndall, Bon Homme County: dwelling 220, family 231, has Ira O. Kinnick, Partner, age 38? (badly smudged), single, born Illinois, father born, Ohio, mother born Illinois, Foreman, trainage gang; in Leacky M. Walsh household.

Note 3: 1920 Soundex has them at 208 East 20th Street, Cheyenne, renting. Farmer, Owner. Actual census sheet has ages 45 and 34, living in a triplex; Election Precinct No. 20, Laramie District, Cheyenne City.

Note 4: Ira O. Kinnick Household, 1930 U. S. Census, population schedule, Wyoming, Laramie County, Cheyenne City, part of Ward 2, dwelling 199, family 219, p. 8B. Ira O. Kinnick, Head, age 54, married first at age 38, born in Illinois, both parents born in Illinois. Occupation: Car Inspector on the Railroad. Wife, Delta M. Kinnick, age 44, married first at age 38, born in Nebraska, father born in Pennsylvania, mother born in Iowa, none listed for occupation.

Note 5: Personal note from Russell & Carolyn (her voice) Stroud, Buda, dated April 18, 1996: "Buda was noted as a R. R. Center and Margaret said Odell Kinnick and Susan Kinnick Hamrick went to Wyoming and worked on the R. R."

Note 6: From obituary of Mary Etta Kinnick Horton, died 6 December 1939, under survivors: "Ira Kinnick, of Cheyenne, Wyoming."

Note 7: World War I Draft Registration Cards, 1917-1918, Wyoming, Laramie County: Ira Odell Kinnick, Paola, age 44, born July 20th, 1874, white, native born, Farmer, Self-employed, Place of Employment: Paola, Laramie County, Wyoming; nearest relative: Delda May Kinnick, Paola, Laramie County, Wyoming; signed; page 2 information: Medium Height, Medium Build, Blue Eyes, Brown Hair; information taken by Harry Farthing, September 12th, 1918. (Ancestry.com)

Note 8: As a youngster, with my family, we did visit Ira and Delda in Cheyenne.

Ira Odell KINNICK and Delda Mae MCCOY were married on 26 Nov 1913.

Delda Mae MCCOY (daughter of Howard MCCOY and Melissa Ann LICHTENWALTER) was born on 17 Jun 1885 in Nebraska. She died on 15 May 1970 in Wyoming.

Note 1: 1920 Soundex says age 34, born in NE, Mother born in IA, Father in PA.

Note 2: Nancy GEDCOM file, May 1998: Birth and marriage date, parents, siblings, first husband name and other information.

Note 3: SSDI has Delda M. Kinnick, b. 17 Jun 1885, d. 15 May 1970, issued Wyo, last res: 82001, Cheyenne, Laramie Co, Wy.

37. **Katherine Susan (Katie) KINNICK** (Walter Watson-2, Susanna (Susan) SCHWYHART-1) was born on 22 Feb 1876 in Buda, Bureau Co, Illinois. She died on 20 Jan 1929 in Greeley, Colorado.

Note 1: Katie Kinnick, her name used in "Buda, Our Home Town, 1828-1975," (1875?) p.202; says birth date 12 Feb 1876, death place. "Buda was the home of the family many years and they went in search of better climate for her health. They were parents of five daughters and three sons." Also, says she has three sisters, Emma, Etta, and Grace, plus two brothers, Ira and George.

Note 2: Living in Diamond, WY, in 1923, per Jacob estate.

Note 3: 1910 census says married 14 years, 10 children, 7 now living.

Note 4: Personal note from Russell & Carolyn (her voice) Stroud, Buda, dated April 18, 1996: "Buda was noted as a R. R. Center and Margaret said Odell Kinnick and Susan Kinnick Hamrick went to Wyoming and worked on the R. R."

Katherine Susan (Katie) KINNICK and Levi HAMRICK were married on 26 Jun 1895 in Kinnick home, Buda, Bureau Co, Illinois.

Levi HAMRICK (son of Christopher HAMRICK and Susan O. SAPP) was born about 1874 in Concord, Bureau Co, Illinois. He died in 1911.

Note 1: In May, 1965, at death of son, Delbert, surviving children listed as Robert of Kewanee, Mrs. Bessie Fisher of Linwood, CA, Mrs. Stella Belanger of Bellfower, CA, Mrs. Clara Belle Adams of Denver, CO, and Mrs. M..... Temple of Westminister, CO

Note 2: Death date from Genealogy.com tree by Don Baldwin <donb@qualcomm.com> 2000.

Katherine Susan (Katie) KINNICK and Levi HAMRICK had the following children:

+130	i.	**Elizabeth D. (Bessie) HAMRICK**, born on 17 Jun 1896, Illinois; died on 3 Apr 1996, Riverside Co, CA.
+131	ii.	**Mary HAMRICK**, born about Jun 1897.
+132	iii.	**Estella Etyle (Stella) HAMRICK**, born on 10 Apr 1899, Illinois; died on 16 Sep 1981, Los Angeles Co, California.
133	iv.	**Guy HAMRICK** was born in Apr 1899 in Illinois.

  Note 1: Guy L. on 1900 and 1910 census, born Apr 1899.
  Note 2: Only brother listed in death notice of Delbert, in May 1965, is Robert
  Note 3: 1930 census has Guy Hamrick as inmate in Illinois State Penitentiary, District 92, Lockport, Will Co, IL, age 31, IL, IL, IL...

+134	v.	**Delbert W. HAMRICK**, born on 19 Sep 1900, Wyanet, Bureau Co, Illinois; married Gertrude LYONS, on 18 Feb 1934, Wyoming; died about 10 May 1965, Kewanee, Henry Co, Illinois.
+135	vi.	**Margaret E. (Margie) HAMRICK**, born about 1902, Illinois; died before May 1965.
136	vii.	**Willard H. HAMRICK** was born about 1907 in Illinois. He died before May 1965.

  Note 1: Willard H., age 3, on 1910 census.
  Note 2: Only brother listed by Delbert in death notice in May 1965 is Robert?!?

Note 3: 1930 census has Willard Hamrick, 23, S, Construction Crew, Sugar Factory, in Johnstown, Weld Co, CO.
Note 4: SSDI, 4 Oct 1906, Apr 1978, Greenville, Madison County, Florida: Willard Hamrick ??

+137   viii.   **Clara Belle HAMRICK**, born on 14 Jun 1908, Illinois; died in Jun 1982.

138   ix.   **Laura Etta HAMRICK** was born on 30 Sep 1909. She died on 30 Oct 1909. She was buried in Forest Hill Cemetery, Wyanet, Bureau Co, Illinois. Death notice

139   x.   **Katherine Mavis HAMRICK** was born about 1910. She died on 22 Jun 1925 in Hopeland Cemetery, Buda, Bureau Co, Illinois.

40. Mary Etta KINNICK (Walter Watson-2, Susanna (Susan) SCHWYHART-1) was born on 17 May 1885 in Buda, Bureau Co, Illinois. She died on 6 Dec 1939. She was buried in Hopeland Cemetery, Buda, Bureau Co, Illinois.
Note 1: Living in Wyanet, IL, in 1923, per Jacob estate; nine children, three died in infancy.
Note 2: 1900 census has Walter, age 59, Day Laborer, with Mary, age 56, and Etta, age 15, and Grace, age 12.

Mary Etta KINNICK and Simon Garfield (Garfield) HORTON were married on 31 Dec 1902 in Buda, Bureau Co, Illinois.

Simon Garfield (Garfield) HORTON (son of Andrew Philip HORTON and Margaret (Maggie) SHARER) was born on 4 Sep 1881 in Milo Township, Bureau Co, Illinois. He died in Sep 1961 in Peoria Hospital, Peoria, Peoria Co, Illinois. He was buried in Hopeland Cemetery, Buda, Bureau Co, Illinois.
Note 1: 1900 census has Garfield living with parents, Andrew and Maggie, age 18.
Note 2: He died as a retired carpenter.
Note 3: Living in Buda, Jan 1944.
Note 4: Garfield Horton of Buda attended funeral of aunt Sarah in July 1905 in Kewanee.
Note 5: Buda Plain Dealer, 9 Jun 1950, has Horton Reunion, "The same officers were appointed: Garfield Horton, president; Mrs. Alvin Smith, vice president; Ralph Horton of Galva, treasurer; and Mrs. Andrew Horton, secretary."
Note 6: 1920 census, Concord Twp, Bureau Co, IL, has Simon G Horton, 38, Laborer??, wife, Mary Etta, 34, son Theodore, 14, son Wilmer, 13, son Thomas, 8, daughter Margaret, 6, son Donald, 3 2/12, son George, 11/12.
Note 7: 1930 census, Buda, Bureau Co, IL, has S. Garfield Horton, 48, first married at 21, IL3, Laborer, Day work for town, with wife, Mary E, 44, first married at 18, IL, OH, IL, and daughter Margaret E, 16 and son Donald F., 13.

Mary Etta KINNICK and Simon Garfield (Garfield) HORTON had the following children:

140   i.   **Theodore HORTON** was born on 13 Nov 1905. He died in Jun 1984.
Note 1: Birth and Death from SS record, LDS files, probably in Princeton.
Note 2: In Canton in 1939, in Princeton in 1961.

141   ii.   **Wilmer J. HORTON** was born on 8 Jan 1907. He died in Feb 1966.
Note 1: Birth and Death from SS record, LDS files, probably in Canton, Fulton Co.

Note 2: In Canton, in 1939, in Canton, in 1961.

142   iii. **Thomas L. HORTON** was born on 14 May 1911. He died on 23 Aug 1989.
Note 1: Birth and Death from SS record, LDS files, died in Kewanee, Henry Co.
Note 2: In Kewanee in 1939, in Princeton, in 1961.
Note 3: In home of Ira and Mary Seyller in 1930 census, age 18:
Note 4: 1930 census, 3 Apr, has John and Gracie in District 10, Canton City, Ward 3, Canton Township, Fulton Co, IL: John, 45, IL, Germ, NY; 22 when first married; Brakeman on Railroad, living on Chestnut Street; with wife, Grace, 42, first married when 19, IL, OH, IL; sharing home with son-in-law, John E. Casson, 24, machinist at plow factory, married first at 23; with his wife, their daughter, Grace, 18, first married at 17; also, son Walter W. Seyller, 15, S, and son Paul K., 10. In next house, son Ira H., 20, first married at 20, with wife, Mary E., 19, first married at 18. Also in their home is Thomas E. Horton, nephew, 18. All these folks were IL, IL, IL.

+143   iv. **Margaret HORTON**, born in 1914.

144   v. **Donald H. HORTON,** born in 1917.
Note 1: Per mother's and father's obits.
Note 2: In Buda in 1939 and "of California, in 1961."
Note 3: 1930 census, Buda, Bureau Co, IL, has S. Garfield Horton, 48, first married at 21, IL3, Laborer, Day work for town, with wife, Mary E, 44, first married at 18, IL, OH, IL, and daughter Margaret E, 16 and son Donald F., 13.

145   vi. **George HORTON** was born in 1919 in Illinois.
Note 1: Per mother's and father's obits.
Note 2: In Buda in 1939, in Kewanee in 1961.
Note 3: Social Security Death Index has born 7 Aug 1922, died Oct 1968.

41. **Gracie Irene KINNICK** (Walter Watson-2, Susanna (Susan) SCHWYHART-1) was born on 30 Oct 1887 in Buda, Bureau Co, Illinois. She died on 29 Dec 1945.
Note 1: Living in Wyanet, IL, in 1923, per Jacob estate
Note 2: Listed in 1920 census as Gracie I, age 32
Note 3: 1900 census has Walter, age 59, Day Laborer, with Mary, age 56, and Etta, age 15, and Grace, age 12.
Note 4: From obituary of Mary Etta Kinnick Horton, died 6 December 1939, under survivors: "Mrs. Grace Seyller, of Galesburg."

Gracie Irene KINNICK and John SEYLLER were married in Jan 1907 in Buda, Bureau Co, Illinois.

John SEYLLER was born about 1884 in Illinois.
Note 1: Had birth year as 1894 - appears in error. 1920 Soundex says 36, she 32. This would make birth year 1884; seems better.
Note 2: 1930 census, 3 Apr, has John and Gracie in District 10, Canton City, Ward 3, Canton Township, Fulton Co, IL: John, 45, IL, Germ, NY; 22 when first married; Brakeman on Railroad, living on Chestnut Street; with wife, Grace, 42, first married when 19, IL, OH, IL;

sharing home with son-in-law, John E. Casson, 24, machinist at plow factory, married first at 23; with his wife, their daughter, Grace, 18, first married at 17; also, son Walter W. Seyller, 15, S, and son Paul K., 10. In next house, son Ira H., 20, first married at 20, with wife, Mary E., 19, first married at 18. Also in their home is Thomas E. Horton, nephew, 18. All these folks were IL, IL, IL.

Gracie Irene KINNICK and John SEYLLER had the following children:

+146	i.	**Ira H. SEYLLER**, born on 17 May 1909, Illinois; married Mary L. UNKNOWN, in 1929; died on 14 May 1969, Orange Co, California.
+147	ii.	**Estella (Grace) SEYLLER**, born about 1912, Illinois.
148	iii.	**Infant SEYLLER** was born about Jan 1914. She died on 1 Feb 1914. She was buried in Hopeland Cemetery, Buda, Bureau Co, Illinois.
+149	iv.	**Walter SEYLLER**, born about 1915, Illinois.
+150	v.	**Paul Kenneth SEYLLER**, born on 29 May 1919, Buda, Bureau Co, Illinois; married Peggy WESTERFIELD, in 1941; died on 1 Oct 1990, Santa Clara Co, California.

42. **Fannie Elizabeth FLETCHER** (Catharine KINNICK-2, Susanna (Susan) SCHWYHART-1) was born on 21 Jul 1860 in Illinois. She died on 30 Jan 1930.
Note 1: Per 1880 Census, Concord Twp, Bureau Co, IL
Note 2: Fannie E. not listed in 1937 obit, when Ora L. died. Obit says twelve siblings. One brother and two sisters preceded Ora. Appears this is the other sister. Susie died as teenager.
Note 3: 1870 census has Fannie age 10, born IL.; 1880 census has Fannie E. age 18?
Note 4: Birth and death dates per Violet letter, 18 Mar 1996.
Note 5: Middle name from probate record of uncle, William Eugene Lyon, 1930.

Fannie Elizabeth FLETCHER and John E. WILLIAMS were married on 28 Feb 1888 in Washington Co, Iowa.

John E. WILLIAMS was born on 21 Mar 1851 in North Wales. He died on 6 Jul 1907 in three mi. n.e.of, Crawfordsville, Washington Co, Iowa.
Note 1: From Brides Reg, Wash Co, IA

Fannie Elizabeth FLETCHER and John E. WILLIAMS had the following children:

151	i.	**Kate WILLIAMS** was born in 1894 in Iowa. (Crawford Twp)
		Note 1: Name per father's obit
+152	ii.	**Alice WILLIAMS**, born on 27 May 1889, Crawfordsville, Washington Co, Iowa; married Wilbert ROSE, on 11 Dec 1912, Crawfordsville, Washington Co, Iowa; died on 19 Feb 1975, Washington Care Center, Washington, Iowa.
153	iii.	**Millie WILLIAMS** was born in 1895 in Iowa. (Crawford Twp)
		Note 1: Name per father's obit

44. **John Townsend (Jack) FLETCHER** (Catharine KINNICK-2, Susanna (Susan) SCHWYHART-1) was born on 28 Nov 1863 near Sheffield, Concord Twp, Bureau Co, Illinois.

He died on 30 Jun 1931 in at home, Crawfordsville, Washington Co, Iowa.

Note 1: Per 1880 Census, Concord Twp, Bureau Co, IL

Note 2: John T not listed in 1937 obit, when Ora L. died. Obit says twelve siblings. One brother and two sisters preceded Ora. Appears this is the brother.

Note 3: 1920 IA census has Washington Co, Crawfordsville, listing for a John, age 55, born in IL. Must be him. Wife, JA, age 53, born IA. Son, Grant, age 17, born in Iowa, and GS (grandson?) Walter Menefee, age 10, born in IA.

Note 4: Middle name Townsend for obit 30 Jun 1931.

Note 5: Had shown daughter - inferred from 1920 census, grandson listing for family of John Wash Co Groom Register has a John Fletcher marrying a Mrs. Laura Wilds Menefee on 10 Jan 1914. This John Fletcher would appear to be a son of John T born about 1890, not a daughter, and the child is a step-grandson of the John T. No, second wife of Jack, no son John, it appears.

Note 6: 1870 census says Jno age 6, 1880 census says John T. age 15.

Note 7: Known as Jack, per Carrie Obit

Note 8: Birth and death from his obit, 1931.

Note 9: Laura Wiles was second wife of Jack, see her obit, 1938.

Note 10: See Violet Lowe letter note on Laura Wiles notes.

Note 11: John T. Fletcher household, 1900 U. S. Census, Iowa, Keokuk County, Richland Township, Dwelling 249, Family 252: John T., Head, Nov 1863, 36, M 12, Illinois, Illinois, Illinois, R. R. Labor; Carrie M., Wife, Nov 1868, (smear), M 12, 5, 5, Ohio, Ohio, New York; Adelia G., Daughter, July 1888, 11, S, Iowa, Illinois, Ohio, At School; Fannie C., Daughter, Sept 1890, 9, S, Iowa, Illinois, Ohio, At School; Joseph, Son, May 1893, 7, S, Iowa, Illinois, Ohio, At School; Ruth H., Daughter, Dec 1896, 3, S, Iowa, Illinois, Ohio; Mazie N., Daughter, Feb 1900, 3/12, S, Iowa, Illinois, Ohio.

John Townsend (Jack) FLETCHER and Carrie May WHYTE were married on 3 Oct 1888 in Crawfordsville, Washington Co, Iowa.

Carrie May WHYTE was born on 19 Nov 1868 in Columbus, Ohio. She died on 13 Mar 1906 in Crawfordsville, Washington Co, Iowa.

Note 1: Per 1920 census, says wife is J.A., Carrie died 1906, J.A. a second wife.

Note 2: Carrie obit says Carrie M. Whyte, Born 19 Nov 1868, Columbus, OH. Jack and Carrie had seven children, all living in Mar 1906 when she died; youngest is "a babe but two weeks old." (but they are not listed!)

John Townsend (Jack) FLETCHER and Carrie May WHYTE had the following children:

+154	i.	**Delia FLETCHER**, born on 14 Jul 1889; died on 23 Jan 1951.
+155	ii.	**Fannie Catherine FLETCHER**, born on 14 Sep 1890, near, Crawfordsville, Washington Co, Iowa; married Warren J. WILLIAMS, on 22 Feb 1911; died on 11 Dec 1917, near, Crawfordsville, Washington Co, Iowa.
156	iii.	**Joseph Allen FLETCHER** was born on 30 May 1893 in Winfield, Iowa. He died on 17 Oct 1919 in Crawfordsville, Washington Co, Iowa. Note 1: Assume dead by Jul 1931, per father's obit Note 2: See obit of Joseph for details. Died age 26
157	iv.	**Ruth Hazel FLETCHER** was born on 16 Dec 1896 in Crawfordsville,

Washington Co, Iowa. She died on 1 Mar 1973 in Washington Care Center, Washington, Washington Co, Iowa. She was buried in Crawfordsville, Washington Co, Iowa.
Note 1: Per her obit; age 76. She was reared in that community (Crawfordsville) and had lived in Washington since 1971. She had been in failing health for a number of years and was seriously ill the past week. Surviving are a sister, Mrs. Ralph Ross of Winfield, a brother, Grant Fletcher, and a number of nieces and nephews.

+158   v.   **Mazie Verlee FLETCHER**, born on 11 Feb 1900; married Ralph Wesley ROSS, on 29 Jan 1919; died on 29 Mar 1989.

+159   vi.   **Grant FLETCHER**, born on 14 Oct 1902, Iowa; married Velma Dorothy ORR, on 1 Sep 1907, Monmouth, Illinois; died on 16 Feb 1974.

John Townsend (Jack) FLETCHER second Laura WILES on 10 Jan 1914.

Laura WILES was born on 2 Jan 1866 in Brighton, Iowa. She died on 18 Dec 1938 in Crawfordsville, Washington Co, Iowa.
Note 1: Second wife of Jack Fletcher. Obit says "she is survived by her son, Homer Menefee of Burlington, a grandson, Walter Menefee, who had lived with her since his mother's death..."
Note 2: Letter from Violet Lowe, 9-14-96, says: Uncle Jack remarried - Laura Wiles - no children. 1 Stepson Homer Menefee, 1 son "Buster" deceased.

46. **Edna Evelyn FLETCHER** (Catharine KINNICK-2, Susanna (Susan) SCHWYHART-1) was born on 6 Nov 1869 in Bureau Co, Illinois. She died on 28 Oct 1946 in County Hospital, Washington, Washington Co, Iowa. She was buried on 30 Oct 1946 in Crawfordsville, Washington Co, Iowa.
Note 1: Per 1880 Census, Concord Twp, Bureau Co, IL
Note 2: Edna (Hull) lived in Williamsburg, KS, in 1937 when Ora L. died; assume this is correct name, not Eduah as in 1880 census typing.
Note 3: Listed in 1920 census, Franklin Co, KS, husband Frank, age 56 (b. OH), with children Blance and Walter.
Note 4: Could not find in 1910 H400 soundex; also, not in Iowa, Crawfordville Twp, Wash. co.
Note 5: 1870 census has Edna, age 7/12; 1880 has Eduah E., age 10.
Note 6: Obit says two sons and one daughter, three grandchildren. "Following marriage, they moved to a farm near Crawfordsville and in 1909 moved to Kansas, where they lived until they returned to Crawfordsville in April, 1944. She was a member of the Williamsburg Methodist church."
Note 7: Birth date, and Frank's years, from Violet 18 May 1996 letter.
Note 8: Additional family information from Evelyn McKittrick, 10 Sep 1996.

Edna Evelyn FLETCHER and Charles Franklin (Frank) HULL were married on 25 Jan 1893 in Iowa.

Charles Franklin (Frank) HULL (son of Moses Aaron HULL and Jane BENNETT) was born on 22 May 1863 in Mt. Vernon, Ohio. He died on 4 Dec 1944 in Crawfordsville, Washington Co, Iowa. He was buried on 7 Dec 1944 in Crawfordsville, Washington Co, Iowa.
Note 1: Edna married to Hull, per Ora L. obit, 1937 Listed in 1920 census. Violet letter says

1863-1944.

Note 2: Details from Evelyn L. McKittrick, 10 Sep 1996. Says moved to Kansas in 1907, when Walter was 5 years old. Purchased farm next to Horne farm.

Edna Evelyn FLETCHER and Charles Franklin (Frank) HULL had the following children:

+160   i. **Blanche Ava HULL**, born on 28 Jan 1896, Crawfordsville, Washington Co, Iowa; married John Wilson HORNE, on 18 Jun 1924, Home/Bride'sPar, Williamsburg, Franklin Co, Kansas; died on 2 Mar 1937, Bell Memorial Hospital, Kansas City, Kansas.

+161   ii. **David Fletcher HULL**, born on 9 Apr 1898, Crawfordsville, Washington Co, Iowa; married Della BROWNING, on 31 Jan 1925, Wapello, Iowa; died on 10 Nov 1982, Washington Co Ho, Washington, Washington Co, Iowa.

+162   iii. **Walter Kinnick HULL**, born on 16 Oct 1902, Crawfordsville, Washington Co, Iowa; married Beryl Alice ANDERSON, on 6 Aug 1923, Butler, Missouri; died on 24 Jul 1977, Colorado Springs, Colorado.

47. **Royal W. FLETCHER** (Catharine KINNICK-2, Susanna (Susan) SCHWYHART-1) was born on 3 Oct 1872 in Sheffield, Illinois. He died about Dec 1948. He was buried in Columbus City Cemetery, Columbus City, Iowa.
Note 1: Per 1880 Census, Concord Twp, Bureau Co, IL
Note 2: Roy lives in Iowa in 1937 when Ora L. died
Note 3: Roy Fletcher appears in 1920 Soundex in rural Louisa Co (is less than four miles east of Crawfordsville IA); age right, lists wife Alice and daughter Hazel.
Note 4: 1900 census lists Roy W. family in Clive Grove Twp, Louisa Co, born Oct 1872, IL., with wife Alice and children, Harry and Pearl, along with a protégé, Bert Lemon, b. Oct 1885, Iowa, age 16, and David Griffith, brother in law (BL), b. May 1878, Iowa, age 22.
Note 5: 1880 census has Royal W. age 7.
Note 6: Roy of Wyman in Mar 1927 per mother's obit
Note 7: In own obit, survived by widow, 15 grandchildren, 15 g-gch, 2 gggch. They lived on farms in the Wyman and Spring Run communities.
Note 8: Death date and place, per Violet 18 May 1996 letter.

Royal W. FLETCHER and Alice GRIFFITH were married on 18 Jun 1891 in Washington Co, Iowa.

Alice GRIFFITH was born about Jun 1871 in Iowa. She died on 18 Jun 1954 in Winfield, Iowa. She was buried in Columbus City, Iowa.
Note 1: Per 1900 census.
Note 2: Last name per Roy's obit; says age 83.

Royal W. FLETCHER and Alice GRIFFITH had the following children:

+163   i. **Harry A. FLETCHER**, born on 6 Feb 1892, Crawfordsville, Washington Co, Iowa; married Hazel Pearl JONES, on 17 Nov 1909, Columbus Junction, Louisa Co, Iowa; died before Nov 1986.

+164   ii. **Pearl M. FLETCHER**, born on 3 Dec 1896, south of, Wyman, Iowa;

married Hilton GIPPLE, on 2 Dec 1919; died on 25 May 1939.

+165   iii.   **Hazel Alice FLETCHER**, born on 15 Jun 1905, Louisa Co, Iowa; married Fred E. KLOPFENSTEIN, on 23 Dec 1925, Washington, Washington Co, Iowa; died on 3 Nov 1986, Henry Co Health Center, Mt. Pleasant, Iowa.

48. Ora Layton FLETCHER (Catharine KINNICK-2, Susanna (Susan) SCHWYHART-1) was born on 20 Oct 1874 in Hickory Grove, Illinois. He died on 29 Jul 1937 in Gold Twp, Bureau Co, Illinois. He was buried in Forest Hill Cemetery, Wyanet, Bureau Co, Illinois.
Note 1: Per Jet Hall 27 Nov 95 Info, birth and death dates
Note 2: Exact death date and place from Bureau Co report # 4, inc probate
Note 3: Have Obit, 1-27-96: ...when a small boy, he went to live with his aunt and uncle, M/M Jacob Kinnick, on a farm north of Sheffield, where he lived until he retired in 1921. At that time he moved to Wyanet, IL, where he lived at the time of his death. His father and mother had moved to IA."
Note 4: 62y, 9m, 9d at death.
Note 5: 1880 census has Ora L age 5.
Note 6: 1910 census, living with Jacob and Fannie Kinnick on farm, wife Rose, children Earl and Rose. Farmer, Gen Farm.

Ora Layton FLETCHER and Rose Ella HALL were married on 19 Dec 1900.

Rose Ella HALL (daughter of Justus (Jet) HALL and Mary MCNEIL) was born on 17 Mar 1877 in Illinois. She died on 20 Jul 1940.
Note 1: Per Jet Hall 27 Nov 95 Info Death date here 1949, earlier had 1940
Note 2: Rose Hall was from New Bedford at time of marriage, per obit of Ora.
Note 3: 1900 Soundex, living with John W. and Lydia (sister) Richmond in Wynanet; says birth was Mar 1871, age 28
Note 4: 1910 census has Rose, age 33, with Ora, age 34, children Earl age 3, Inea, age 2/12. Says married 9 years, 3 children, 2 living.
Note 5: Birth and Death dates per Violet letter 18 May 1996.

Ora Layton FLETCHER and Rose Ella HALL had the following children:

166   i.   **Fannie Ann FLETCHER** was born on 27 Apr 1902. She died on 19 Jun 1902.
       Note 1: Per Jet Hall 27 Nov 95 Info, name, death date
       Note 2: Exact birth and death date from Bureau Co report # 4, inc probate
+167   ii.   **Earl R. FLETCHER**, born on 3 May 1906.
+168   iii.   **Inez Nellie FLETCHER**, born on 28 Jan 1910.

49. Samuel Clinton (Clint) FLETCHER (Catharine KINNICK-2, Susanna (Susan) SCHWYHART-1) was born on 19 Jan 1877 in Bureau Co, Illinois. He died on 22 Oct 1953 in Crawfordsville, Washington Co, Iowa. He was buried on 25 Oct 1953 in New Cemetery, Crawfordsville, Washington Co, Iowa.
Note 1: Per 1880 Census, Concord Twp, Bureau Co, IL
Note 2: Clinton lives in Iowa in 1937 when Ora L. died
Note 3: Based on 1900 and 1920 census soundex records, appears to be using initials, S.C. rather

than Clinton. Assuming this is him, he is 23, in Henry Co, IA, Jefferson Twp, City of Wayland, living alone, in 1900. In 1920, he is back in Crawfordsville, Washington Co, with wife, DA, age 38, b. IA; daughter, DI, age 9, and son, CC, age 4, both born in IA.
Note 4: S. Clint on cemetery record
Note 5: 1880 census has Clinton age 3.
Note 6: Obit: age 76, auto dealer and civic community leader in Crawfordsville; came to Washington County when he was seven years old; 4 grand children.
Note 7: Per Wife's obit, Jan 1956, M/M "moved to Wayland (Henry Co) following their marriage and lived there for about a year before moving to Crawfordsville which had been their home since 1901. 5 grand children survive
Note 8: Marriage date per Violet letter 18 Mar 1996.

Samuel Clinton (Clint) FLETCHER and Delia Anna HULL were married on 19 Dec 1900 in Muscatine, Iowa.

Delia Anna HULL (daughter of Moses HULL) was born on 2 Sep 1881 in near, Crawfordsville, Washington Co, Iowa. She died on 25 Jan 1956. She was buried in New Cemetery, Crawfordsville, Washington Co, Iowa.
Note 1: Per 1920 census cemetery - 1881

Samuel Clinton (Clint) FLETCHER and Delia Anna HULL had the following children:

169		i.	**Max Eugene FLETCHER** was born on 11 Mar 1909. He died on 28 Mar 1909. Note 1: Per father's obit, infant son, Max Eugene, died in infancy. Note 2: Dates from Evelyn L. McKittrick, 10 Sep 1996.
+170		ii.	**Doris Irene FLETCHER**, born on 9 Aug 1910, Crawfordsville, Washington Co, Iowa; married Kenneth Harper CHERRYHOLMES, on 23 Jun 1928, Methodist Parsonage, Crawfordsville, Washington Co, Iowa; died on 7 Dec 1952, Crawfordsville, Washington Co, Iowa.
+171		iii.	**Cleo Clinton FLETCHER**, born on 21 Jun 1915, Iowa; married Arlene LOWE, on 29 Aug 1936, Knoxville, Iowa; died on 21 Jan 1970.

50. Frank William FLETCHER (Catharine KINNICK-2, Susanna (Susan) SCHWYHART-1) was born on 9 Dec 1878 in Bureau Co, Illinois. He died on 5 Mar 1955 in University Hosp, Iowa City, Johnson Co, Iowa. He was buried on 7 Mar 1955 in New Cemetery, Crawfordsville, Washington Co, Iowa.
Note 1: Per 1880 Census, Concord Twp, Bureau Co, IL
Note 2: Frank lived in Iowa in 1937 when Ora L. died
Note 3: Frank Fletcher appears in 1920 Soundex in Crawfordsville on Vine St; is correct age, assume is the right one; wife and kids from Soundex card. (mid-Cont 1-27-96)
Note 4: 1900 Soundex says birth Dec 1878, Frank W.
Note 5: 1880 census has Frank W age 1.
Note 6: Obit says birth 9 Dec 1878; died age 76. All six children survive, 15 gch, 2 g-gch, 2 sisters, Grace and Nellie and one brother, Eugene of Wapello. Frank was street commissioner of Crawfordsville for 28 years.

Frank William FLETCHER and Jessie Luella MITCHELL were married on 6 Feb 1907 in Crawfordsville, Washington Co, Iowa.

Jessie Luella MITCHELL (daughter of James L. MITCHELL and Martha H. PALMER) was born on 5 Feb 1888 in Crawford Twp, Washington Co, Iowa. She died on 29 Mar 1951 in at home, Crawfordsville, Washington Co, Iowa. She was buried on 31 Mar 1951 in New Cemetery, Crawfordsville, Washington Co, Iowa.
Note 1: Life-long resident of the Crawfordsville comm. Survived by her husband, all six children, five brothers, 12 gch.

Frank William FLETCHER and Jessie Luella MITCHELL had the following children:

+172   i. **Vernon Guy FLETCHER**, born on 18 Apr 1908, Iowa; married Ruthe Austin HAMMOND, on 2 Nov 1940, Ft. Madison, Iowa; died on 7 Apr 1980, Crawfordsville, Washington Co, Iowa.

+173   ii. **John Lyle (Lyle) FLETCHER**, born on 9 May 1910, Iowa; married Ione FROST, on 18 Jun 1955, Kahoka, Missouri; married Grace FITZGERALD, on 5 Nov 1932; died on 2 Jan 1987, Sherrard, Illinois.

174   iii. **William Virgil "Dutch" FLETCHER** was born on 1 Jun 1912 in Crawfordsville, Washington Co, Iowa. He died on 27 Jan 1985 in Washington County Hospital, Washington, Washington Co, Iowa. He was buried in New Cemetery, Crawfordsville, Washington Co, Iowa.
Note 1: Virgil of Crawfordsville, Mar 1951, when mother died.
Note 2: Per Vernon obit, Apr 1980, Virgil of Crawfordsville.
Note 3: Per own obit, Jan 1985, known as "Dutch." He never married and spent his entire life in this area (Crawfordsville); survived by a bro, Lyle, of Sherrard, IL, and 2 sis, Lois (Mrs. Dell) Farrier, Columbus Junction, and Violet (Mrs. Delbert) Lowe, Brighton. He had farmed and worked as a carpenter for the Wayland Carpenter Shop until his retirement. He had been ill for the past 30 days but death was unexpected. He was a member of the Presbyterian Church.

+175   iv. **Clarence Arthur FLETCHER**, born on 6 Feb 1915, Iowa; married Olive Jean (Jean) KELSEY, on 3 Sep 1937, Washington Co, Iowa; died on 12 Dec 1972, Moline, Illinois.

+176   v. **Lois Fern FLETCHER**, born on 8 Jul 1920, Crawfordsville, Washington Co, Iowa; married Dell Phillip FARRIER, on 29 Jun 1940, Little Bit O' He, Davenport, Iowa.

+177   vi. **Violet May FLETCHER**, born on 1 May 1924, Crawfordsville, Washington Co, Iowa; married Delbert C. LOWE, on 23 Jan 1947, Brighton, Washington Co, Iowa.

52. Clark Eugene FLETCHER (Catharine KINNICK-2, Susanna (Susan) SCHWYHART-1) was born on 6 May 1883 in Bureau Co, Illinois. He died on 16 Feb 1966. He was buried in New Cemetery, Crawfordsville, Washington Co, Iowa.
Note 1: Eugene lived in Iowa in 1937, when Ora L. died; this is first knowledge of him.
Note 2: Obit says twelve siblings. One brother and two sisters preceded Ora.

Note 3: Estimated birth date and place from relation ship with two youngest girls and move to Iowa

Note 4: 1900 census lists Clark E., born Aug 1883, IL.

Note 5: Lived in Columbus Junction in May 1927 when mother died.

Note 6: His obit says born 6 May 1883; survived by 10 gch, 10 g-gch.

Clark Eugene FLETCHER and Mame CHERRYHOLMES were married on 11 Apr 1906 in Crawfordsville, Washington Co, Iowa.

Mame CHERRYHOLMES (daughter of Harlan Deamuth CHERRYHOLMES and Jennie Rebecca CROOKS) was born on 5 Jul 1888. She died on 15 Sep 1964 in Burlington, Iowa. She was buried on 17 Sep 1964 in Crawfordsville, Washington Co, Iowa.

Note 1: Per obit, survived by 10 gch.

Note 2: Birth year per Violet letter, 18 May 1996.

Note 3: Birth month and day from email 27 Mar 2000 from Stefanie Richardson, Tempe, AZ

Clark Eugene FLETCHER and Mame CHERRYHOLMES had the following children:

+178	i.	**Harlan FLETCHER**, born on 19 Oct 1906; died on 25 Jun 1970.
+179	ii.	**Knowlton FLETCHER**, born in 1911, Iowa.
+180	iii.	**Richard FLETCHER**, born on 4 Jun 1913; died on 15 Mar 1978.

54. **Harry E. WEISE** (Margaret (Maggie) KINNICK-2, Susanna (Susan) SCHWYHART-1) was born in Sep 1872 in Illinois. He died after 1930.

Note 1: Living at 432 South Franklin St., South Bend, IN, in 1923, per Jacob estate.

Note 2: Lived at Inglewood P.O. Box 135, Los Angeles, CA, in 1911, when father died.

Note 3: A Harry Wise is listed in 1897-98 Princeton City Directory, car trim, res 908 n First St., would have been 20+ Jacob had one child in 1877 voters list, WS#6.

Note 4: 1900 census has Harry E., at home with parents, age 27, b. Sep 1872. Also, says Married, for 5 yrs?? No mention of wife.

Note 5: 1930 census for Columbus, Franklin Co, OH, 375 Fifth Street, dwelling187, family187, has Harry E Weise, 38, Div, IL, NJ, IL, Laborer, Hotel

Harry E. WEISE and La Adell "Ella" MARTIN were married on 24 Dec 1899 in Harvey, Illinois.

La Adell "Ella" MARTIN was born in Feb 1874 in Illinois.

Note 1: From Weise Genealogy, per David Weise letter, 19 Mar 1996.

Note 2: 1900 U. S. Census, Illinois, Cook County, Thornton Township, Harvey City, p. 14A, dwelling 235, family 271, Lazenfeld Martin Household, has daughter: Ella M. Weise, Feb 1874, age 26, Married, once, no children, none living. Occupation: Compositor.

Note 3: 1920 U. S. Census, California, Los Angeles County, Inglewood, p.14B, dwelling 110, family 142, Ella M. Martin, age 45, widowed, with son, Frank, age 17.

Note 4: 1930 U. S. census, population schedule, California, Los Angeles County, part of Inglewood City/Township, p. 9B, 4559 Pine, dwelling 140, family 140. Ella, female, age 56, divorced, first married at age 23, born in Illinois, waitress in a café, with son, Frank C., age 27, single, born in Illinois, father born in Illinois, mother born in Illinois, working as automobile salesman.

Harry E. WEISE and La Adell "Ella" MARTIN had the following children:

181   i.   **Frank Clifford WEISE** was born on 24 Dec 1900 in Wyanet, Bureau Co, Illinois.
Note 1: From Weise Genealogy, per David Weise letter, 19 Mar 1996.
Note 2: California Death Index, 1940-1997: (May 2005, Ancestry)

Name:	WEISE, FRANK C
Social Security #:	552093560
Sex:	MALE
Birth Date:	23 Dec 1902
Birthplace:	ILLINOIS
Death Date:	15 Aug 1977
Death Place:	LOS ANGELES

55. Roy E. WEISE (Margaret (Maggie) KINNICK-2, Susanna (Susan) SCHWYHART-1) was born on 12 Aug 1881. He died on 25 Feb 1946 in Harvey, Illinois. He was buried on 28 Feb 1946 in Forest Hill Cemetery, Wyanet, Bureau Co, Illinois.
Note 1: Living in Wyanet, IL, in 1923, per Jacob estate.
Note 2: In Wyanet, 1911, when father died.
Note 3: Cemetery record has birth and death dates.
Note 4: Ray at home with parents in 1900 census, age 18.
Note 5: 1920 census has Roy and Lucy and family in Wyanet.
Note 6: 1910 Miracode has children William, age 5, Florence, age 3, and Lucy NR. No 1910 tape at MC 2-17-96 - box empty!
Note 7: Info from David Weise, 19 Mar 1996, Roy and Lucy died in Harvey, IL.
Note 8: Burial date from Maxine Trotter letter rec'd 4-21-96, from THE WYANET RECORD of March 7, 1946.
Note 9: A ROBERT had been added per Maxine Trotter letter rec'd 21 Apr 1996 quoting THE WYANET RECORD dated March 7, 1946. States a surviving son was "Robert of Harvey."
Note 10: However, in the 1930 census, Maxine is the youngest childe, at age 9, and Lucy is 47 years old... not likely to have another child; deleted the ROBERT.
Note 11: Roy E. Weise Household, 1910 U. S. Census, population schedule, King Street, Wyanet Town, Bureau County, Illinois, p. 4B, dwelling 106, family 110, has Roy E., age 28, first marriage, 7 years, born Illinois, father born in New Jersey, mother born in Illinois, Laborer, Odd jobs, with wife, Lucy E., age 26, first marriage, 7 years, four children, three alive and listed, she and both parents born in Illinois, with children (all single, all born Illinois), son William R., age 5, daughter Florence E, age 3, and Lucy M., age 1 3/12
Note 12: Roy Weise Household, 1920 U. S. Census, population schedule, p 2A, Wyanet village, Bureau County, Illinois, dwelling 37, family 37, has: Roy, age 38, born Illinois, father born New Jersey, mother born Pennsylvania, with wife, Lucy, age 36, she and both parents born in Illinois, with children (each single, born in Illinois), daughter, Florence, age 12, daughter, Mavis, 10, daughter, Blanche, age 9, daughter, Bessie, age 6, Earl, age 4 11/12, and son Harold, age 2 8/12.

Roy E. WEISE and Lucy E. WHITTEN were married – no details available – more information sought

Lucy E. WHITTEN (daughter of Dave WHITTEN and Elizabeth DAGGER) was born on 4 Jul 1883 in Wyanet, Bureau Co, Illinois. She died on 15 Feb 1957 in Harvey, Illinois. She was buried in Forest Hill Cemetery, Wyanet, Bureau Co, Illinois.
Note 1: Per cemetery record,
Note 2: From Our Town, a History of Wyanet: Mr. Dave Whitten was one of these early homesteaders. His daughter was Mrs. Roy (Lucy) Weise, and she was resident on King St. for many years.
Note 3: Birth and death place from Weise Genealogy, per David Weise letter, 19 Mar 1996.
Note 4: 1930 Census, Wyanet, Bureau Co, IL, has Roy L. and Lucy E Weise, 48 and 47, he M21, She M20, he IL, NJ, IL, she IL3, he Laborer, Odd jobs, and (on next page), daughter, Bessie L., 16, son Earl E, 15, son Harold R, 13, and daughter, Maxine D, 7.

Roy E. WEISE and Lucy E. WHITTEN had the following children:

+182	i.	**William WEISE**, born on 17 Feb 1905, Wyanet, Bureau Co, Illinois.
+183	ii.	**Florence Elizabeth WEISE**, born on 25 Mar 1907, Wyanet, Bureau Co, Illinois; married Lloyd FLEENER, in 1925; died in 1990.
+184	iii.	**Lucy Mavis WEISE**, born on 26 Jan 1909, Wyanet, Bureau Co, Illinois; died in 1991.
+185	iv.	**Blanch Janith WEISE**, born on 22 Nov 1911, Wyanet, Bureau Co, Illinois; died on 4 Jul 1975, San Bernadino Co, CA.
+186	v.	**Bessie Lucille WEISE**, born on 6 Apr 1913, Wyanet, Bureau Co, Illinois; died on 1 Jan 1984, California.
+187	vi.	**David Earl (Earl) WEISE**, born on 13 Feb 1915, Wyanet, Bureau Co, Illinois; married Carol(e) Marian (Carole) LONG, on 13 Apr 1941; died on 23 Dec 2004, Turlock, Stanislaus County, California.
+188	vii.	**Harold Roy (Harold) WEISE**, born on 19 Apr 1917, Wyanet, Bureau Co, Illinois.
+189	viii.	**Doris Maxine (Maxine) WEISE**, born on 6 Dec 1922.

Chapter 4

Sarah SCHWYHART and Her Descendants

First Generation

1. **Sarah E. SCHWYHART** was born in 1813. She died in 1899.
Note 1: Per email from Dana Weeden, 11/15/98: see comments in husband's notes and four children noted.
Note 2: Sarah known as Sally? I will assume so. Jul 30, 1999.

Sarah E. SCHWYHART and John Hanson WEEDON were married about 20 Apr 1832 in Belmont Co, Ohio.

John Hanson WEEDON (son of Thomas WEEDON and Letitia PENN) was born about 1810. He died about 1847.
Note 1: Per email from Dana Weeden, 11/15/98: John was my husband's great-great-grandfather's brother and I have some additional information to add on this line. John died sometime in late 1847 or early 1848 and Sarah remarried. I have copies of the marriage license for both of Sarah's marriages, copies of Sarah's application for Widow's pension, and an article published 1895 featuring Sarah's son Alfred.
Note 2: Guernsey Co Historical Sketches, p. 239-40: John became a hatter by trade, making both silk and beaver hats. The family moved to Kimbolton in 1837.
Note 3: Weedon packet from Dana, Nov 18, 1998: more detail of life and death!

Sarah E. SCHWYHART and John Hanson WEEDON had the following children:

+2	i.	**Susan WEEDON**, born about 1833; married Jonathan JONES, Jefferson Co.
+3	ii.	**Joseph T. WEEDEN**, born on 28 Sep 1834, Summerton Co, Ohio; died on 14 Oct 1882.
+4	iii.	**Alfred WEEDON**, born on 15 Nov 1836, Morristown, Belmont Co, Ohio; married Eliza Jane DULL, on 13 Feb 1864; married Emily (Emma) LITTLE, on 1 Jan 1873, Kimbolton, Ohio; married Sarah HILL, on 13 Oct 1879/80; died on 10 Mar 1925, Cambridge.
5	iv.	**Elizabeth E. WEEDON** – more information sought Note 1: Per email from Dana Weeden, 11/15/98: Elizabeth E. Weedon - died in infancy.
6	v.	**John WEEDON** – more information sought Note 1: Per email from Dana Weeden, 11/15/98: name not mentioned.
7	vi.	**Thomas WEEDON** – more information sought. Note 1: Per email from Dana Weeden, 11/15/98: name not mentioned Could be person now listed as Joseph T. Weeden. ??

Second Generation

2. Susan WEEDON (Sarah E. SCHWYHART-1) was born about 1833.
Note 1: Weedon packet from Dana, Nov 18, 1998: born between 1832 and beginning of 1834.

Susan WEEDON and Jonathan JONES were married in Jefferson Co.

Jonathan JONES – more information sought

Note 1: Per email from Dana Weeden, 11/15/98.

3. Joseph T. WEEDEN (Sarah E. SCHWYHART-1) was born on 28 Sep 1834 in Summerton Co, Ohio. He died on 14 Oct 1882. He was buried in Sutton Valley Cemetery, Greeley, Kansas.
Note 1: Per email from Dana Weeden, 11/15/98: Joseph T. Weeden - b. Sep 28, 1834 in Summerton Co., OH d. Oct. 14, 1882. Joseph served as the Sugar Valley postmaster in Anderson County, KS (ca. 1876) elected as Justice of the Peace for Waker Township in 1873. He is buried in the Sutton Valley Cemetery, Greeley, KS.
Note 2: Information sought on marriage.

4. Alfred WEEDON (Sarah E. SCHWYHART-1) was born on 15 Nov 1836 in Morristown, Belmont Co, Ohio. He died on 10 Mar 1925 in Cambridge.
Note 1: Alfred and Eliza Weedon moved to Adair Co, IA, in 1868; later going on to Crawford Co, KS, where Elizabeth died leaving three small children.
Note 2: In 1872 Alfred brought his family back to Guernsey Co. Alfred served as Clerk of the Courts for 6 1/2 years, and as Civil War Pension Agent for a number of years.
Note 3: Per email from Dana Weeden, 11/15/98: b. Nov. 15, 1836 in Morristown, Belmont Co, OH; died Mar. 10, 1925 in Cambridge. Alfred had 3 wives: Eliza J. Dull, Emily Little, and Sarah Hill.

Alfred WEEDON and Eliza Jane DULL were married on 13 Feb 1864.

Eliza Jane DULL (daughter of David DULL and Charlotte Margaret MARTEL) was born.
Alfred WEEDON and Eliza Jane DULL had the following children:

+8	i.	**Ella Nora WEEDON**, born on 15 Oct 1864; married John H. MARLING, on 15 Apr 1885, Guernsey Co, Ohio.
+9	ii.	**Susan Matilda WEEDON**, born in 1868; married A. Maywood MATHEWS, on 21 Nov 1885, Guernsey Co, Ohio.
10	iii.	**David WEEDON** was born in Nov 1869 in Ohio.

> Note 1: Weedon packet from Dana, Nov 18, 1998: Listed as third child; said to be a printer in Seattle, WA.
> Note 2: Listed as D.T. Weedon, 10, in 1880 census, with his parents, and siblings.
> Note 3: Jul 1900 census of Military and Naval Population: Philippine Islands, San Pedro Macati, 4th Infantry: David T. Weedon, Cambridge,

Ohio, Ninth, South, Sergeant, b. Nov 1869, IA OH OH, 30 S.

Alfred WEEDON and Emily (Emma) LITTLE were married on 1 Jan 1873 in Kimbolton, Ohio.

Emily (Emma) LITTLE – more information sought
Note 1: Per email from Dana Weeden, 11/15/98: second wife

Alfred WEEDON and Emily (Emma) LITTLE had the following children:

11	i.	**John F. WEEDON** was born on 25 Jul 1874.
		Note 1: Weedon packet from Dana, Nov 18, 1998:
12	ii.	**Olive M. WEEDON** was born before Mar 1879.
		Note 1: Weedon packet from Dana, Nov 18, 1998:

Alfred WEEDON and Sarah HILL were married on 13 Oct 1879/80.

Sarah HILL was born on 19 Nov 1840 in Ohio. She died on 10 Mar 1936 in Cambridge, Ohio. She was buried in Northwood Cemetery.
Note 1: Guernsey Co Historical Sketches, p. 239-40: third wife

Alfred WEEDON and Sarah HILL had the following children:

13	i.	**Homer H. WEEDON** was born on 9 Oct 1881. He died on 15 Sep 1970 in Dexter City, Noble Co, Ohio.
		Note 1: Weedon packet from Dana, Nov 18, 1998:

Third Generation

8. **Ella Nora WEEDON** (Alfred-2, Sarah E. SCHWYHART-1) was born on 15 Oct 1864.
Note 1: Weedon packet from Dana, Nov 18, 1998: birth date and marriage details.

Ella Nora WEEDON and John H. MARLING were married on 15 Apr 1885 in Guernsey Co, Ohio.

John H. MARLING was born in 1861. He died in 1926.
Note 1: Weedon packet from Dana, Nov 18, 1998:

Ella Nora WEEDON and John H. MARLING had the following children:

+14	i.	**Lucille Lenore MARLING**, born about 1886.
15	ii.	**Paul E. MARLING** was born on 5 Sep 1887. He died on 25 Mar 1982 in Cincinnati, Hamilton Co, Ohio.
		Note 1: Weedon packet from Dana, Nov 18, 1998:
16	iii.	**Arthur Weedon MARLING** was born on 10 Feb 1890. He died on 30 Jul 1967 in Zanesville, Muskingum Co, Ohio.

Note 1: Weedon packet from Dana, Nov 18, 1998:

17   iv.   **Ella MARLING** was born.

Note 1: Weedon packet from Dana, Nov 18, 1998:

18   v.   **Margaret MARLING** was born.

Note 1: Weedon packet from Dana, Nov 18, 1998:

9. **Susan Matilda WEEDON** (Alfred-2, Sarah E. SCHWYHART-1) was born in 1868.
Note 1: Weedon packet from Dana, Nov 18, 1998: middle name and birth year; also marriage.

Susan Matilda WEEDON and A. Maywood MATHEWS were married on 21 Nov 1885 in Guernsey Co, Ohio.

A. Maywood MATHEWS – more information sought
Note 1: Weedon packet from Dana, Nov 18, 1998:

Chapter 5

John SCHWYHART and His Descendants

First Generation

1. **John SCHWYHART** was born on 16 Jan 1818 in Belmont Co, Ohio. He died on 13 Apr 1883 in Adair Co, Iowa. He was buried in North Oak Grove.
Note 1: Per LDS Ancestral File
Note 2: Birth county and state Per Rebecca Fraas, email Nov 1999.

John SCHWYHART and Margaret STONER were married about 1835.

Margaret STONER was born in 1816. She was buried in North Oak Grove.
Note 1: Per LDS Ancestral File
Note 2: Stoner and 1816 per Rebecca Fraas, Nov 1999 email.

John SCHWYHART and Margaret STONER had the following children:

+2	i.	**Rachel Ann SCHWYHART**, born in Jul 1836, Ohio; died on 29 May 1929, Park County, Montana.
3	ii.	**John SCHWYHART** was born on 28 Oct 1838. Note 1: Per LDS Ancestral File
+4	iii.	**Elizabeth SCHWYHART**, born on 21 Jun 1843, Ohio; married Jarius STOREY, on 25 Apr 1867, Kewanee, Henry Co, Illinois; died on 11 May 1904, Kewanee, Henry Co, Illinois.
5	iv.	**Walter SCHWYHART** was born on 16 Apr 1845. Note 1: Per LDS Ancestral File
+6	v.	**Jacob SCHWYHART**, born on 2 Nov 1847, Ohio.
7	vi.	**Mary SCHWYHART** was born on 20 Aug 1850. Note 1: Per LDS Ancestral File
8	vii.	**Sarah SCHWYHART** was born on 3 Apr 1852. Note 1: Per LDS Ancestral File
+9	viii.	**Susan SCHWYHART**, born on 24 Oct 1854, Illinois; married Hiram Adelbert VAN_AKEN, on 23 Dec 1869, Annawa Co, Illinois; died on 19 Apr 1932, Hillsboro, Washington Co, Oregon.

Second Generation

2. **Rachel Ann SCHWYHART** (John-1) was born in Jul 1836 in Ohio. She died on 29 May 1929 in Park County, Montana. She was buried in 1929 in Chico Cemetery, Mill Creek, Park Co, Montana.
Note 1: Death date, per Montana Death Index, 1907-2002 (ancestry.com), Park Co.

Note 2: 1900 census for Park Co, MT, Precinct No. 14, South Cascade, has Rachel, with son, Wm. H, and grandson, Mark, age 63, Widowed, one child, living, b. OH, father and mother b. OH; Farmer, own farm.

Note 3: 1920 census, Rachel is in home of grandson, Mark. She is age 84, b. OH (both parents b. OH).

Note 4: R.A. Edick, age 61 (Jan 1897, therefore, b. 1836), of Red Lodge, Carbon Co, MT (Red Lodge was in Park Co in 1893...), had statement in pension file of Joseph Kinnick, saying she had known Joseph 35 years (1864).

Note 1: Per Rebecca Fraas, email Nov 1999 (& death year and cemetery): last name is Schwyhart!!!

Alonzo P. (Lon) EDICK (son of Mark EDICK and Nancy UNKNOWN) was born between 1823 and 1825 in New York.

Note 1: Resident of Red Lodge, Park Co, MT, in Oct 1893, when he made statement I found in pension file of Joseph Kinnick. Said he had known Joseph (b. Mar 1839) since he was 14 years old (i.e., 1853). Also, said he visited Joseph in 1863, in hospital.

Note 2: 1860 census has Alonzo P., age 36, Rachel, age 24, and William H., age 4, b. IL, along with, in the household: E.B. Wilcox, age 29, Mason, b. NY; in Princeton, Bureau Co, IL.

Note 3: Assume Mark Edick on 1870 census, in Princeton, is father.

Note 4: 1870 census has Alonzo, Rachel, and Wm. H., in Harrison Twp, Adair Co, IA, Dexter P.O., with Van Aken next door and Walter and Mary E. Kinnick in the next house, where Alonzo P. Kinnick was born in 1870.........

Rachel Ann SCHWYHART and Alonzo P. (Lon) EDICK had the following children:

+10   i.   **William H. (Bill) EDICK**, born in Jan 1856, Illinois; married Margaret Susana (Maggie) KINNICK, on 13 Apr 1882, Greenfield, Adair Co, Iowa; died on 28 Jan 1934, Mill Creek, Park County, Montana.

4. **Elizabeth SCHWYHART** (John-1) was born on 21 Jun 1843 in Ohio. She died on 11 May 1904 in Kewanee, Henry Co, Illinois. She was buried in Henry Co, Illinois.

Note 1: Per LDS Ancestral File

Note 2: Per Judith K. Vermilion, 11 Oct 1998: Death and burial information. Further, apparently divorced from Jarius by 27 Feb 1872, when he married Nancy Dingman.

Elizabeth SCHWYHART and Jarius STOREY were married on 25 Apr 1867 in Kewanee, Henry Co, Illinois.

Jarius STOREY (son of Elijah STOREY and Louise WHEELER) was born on 18 Mar 1828 in Oneida Co, New York. He died on 24 Dec 1911 in Kewanee, Henry Co, Illinois. He was buried in Kewanee, Henry Co, Illinois.

Note 1: Per Judith K. Vermilion, 11 Oct 1998: All; other marriage, 27 Feb 1872 - Nancy Dingman. (He and Elizabeth presumably had divorced by then!)

Elizabeth SCHWYHART and Jarius STOREY had the following children:

11   i.   **Baby Boy STOREY** was born in Henry Co, Illinois.

+12   ii.   **Tessa STOREY**, born on 14 Oct 1871, Kewanee, Henry Co, Illinois; married Frederick Arrored REILLY, on 1 May 1906, Kewanee, Henry Co, Illinois; died on 3 Apr 1952, Kewanee, Henry Co, Illinois.

6. **Jacob SCHWYHART** (John-1) was born on 2 Nov 1847 in Ohio.
Note 1: Per LDS Ancestral File
Note 2: 1870 Census, Pesotum Twp, Champaign Co, IA.(has to be Illinois!)
Note 3: 1880 Census, Harrison Twp, Adair Co, IA (30 Jun).

Jacob SCHWYHART and Mae UNKNOWN were married – more information sought

Mae UNKNOWN was born in 1849 in Ohio.
Note 1: 1870 Census, Pesotum Twp, Champaign Co, IA. (has to be Illinois!)
Note 2: 1880 Census, Harrison Twp, Adair Co, IA (30 Jun).

Jacob SCHWYHART and Mae UNKNOWN had the following children:

13   i.   **Charlie SCHWYHART** was born in 1869.
1870 Census, Pesotum Twp, Champaign Co, IA.1880 Census, Harrison Twp, Adair Co, IA (30 Jun).

9. **Susan SCHWYHART** (John-1) was born on 24 Oct 1854 in Illinois. She died on 19 Apr 1932 in Hillsboro, Washington Co, Oregon. She was buried in Forest Grove Cemetery, Forest Grove, Oregon.
Note 1: Per LDS Ancestral File
Note 2: Death information per Rebecca Fraas, email, Nov 1999
Note 3: Tess added town on death
Note 4: See Susan, 76, in Portland with daughter, Lu, in 1930 census!

Susan SCHWYHART and Hiram Adelbert VAN_AKEN were married on 23 Dec 1869 in Annawa Co, Illinois.

Hiram Adelbert VAN_AKEN (son of Francis VAN_AKEN and Mary Ann CAMPBELL) was born on 11 Dec 1851 in Hume, New York. He died on 8 Jan 1928 in Hillsboro, Washington Co, Oregon.
Note 1: Per Rebecca Fraas, Nov 1999 email; marriage info.
Note 2: 1870 census (28 Jul), Dexter P.O., Harrison Twp, Adair Co, IA, has: Herman (looks like) Van Aken, 19, and wife, Susan, living of farm between Walter and Mary E. Kinnick and Alonzo and Rachel Edick, and their son, William H. Edick!
Note 3: 1880 soundex IA, Adair Co, Harrison Twp, wife, Susan, 20, IL; D, 10, IA, L.M. 7 IA, Nellie, 2, IA
Note 4: Tess has middle name, birthday (in New York, not Ohio), death date and marriage info

Susan SCHWYHART and Hiram Adelbert VAN_AKEN had the following children:

+14   i.   **Rosetta VAN_AKEN**, born on 26 Oct 1870, Iowa; married Niels Christian

NIELSON; died on 8 Jul 1955, Hillsboro, Washington Co, Oregon.

+15   ii.   **LuLu Mae VAN_AKEN**, born in 1873, Iowa; married August W. WURL, in 1892; died Portland, Multnomah Co, Oregon.

16   iii.   **Nellie VAN_AKEN** was born in 1878 in Iowa.
Note 1: Per Rebecca Fraas, Nov 1999 email.
Note 2: 1880 Soundex, with parents, Nellie, 2, IA

+17   iv.   **John Jay VAN_AKEN**, born on 16 Sep 1880, Stuart, Guthrie Co, Iowa; died on 8 Mar 1967, Livingston, Park Co, Montana.

+18   v.   **Frank Adelbert VAN_AKEN**, born on 13 Nov 1893, Nebraska; died on 11 Feb 1970, Forest Grove, Washington Co, Oregon.

Third Generation

10.   **William H. (Bill) EDICK** (Rachel Ann SCHWYHART-2, John-1) was born in Jan 1856 in Illinois. He died on 28 Jan 1934 in Mill Creek, Park County, Montana.
Note 1: Marriage record found in Greenfield, IA, Library, 10-7-95 (Nancy)
Note 2: 1900 census, Park Co, MT, divorced, age 44, living with his mother and son, Mark, age 12; born Jan 1856, IL, father b. NY, mother b. OH. Engineer (Station, I believe it says).
Note 3: Death year and place Per Rebecca Fraas, email Nov 1999. Also: (Bill and Maggie) moved to Mill Creek, Park County, MT, in 1889 following Lon and Rachel Ann Edick's move to Mill Creek in 1885. Mark is Lon and Rachel Ann's Grandson. Mark has a brother, Verner, and a sister Nellie.
Note 4: They are 2nd cousins!
Note 5: Montana Death Index, 1907-2002, has William H Edick, Death date: 28 Jan 1934

William H. (Bill) EDICK and Margaret Susana (Maggie) KINNICK were married on 13 Apr 1882 in Greenfield, Adair Co, Iowa.

Margaret Susana (Maggie) KINNICK (daughter of Joseph KINNICK and Rachel Ann MERCER) was born on 5 Jan 1863 in Bureau Co, Illinois. She died on 23 Aug 1951 in Mill Creek, Park County, Montana.
Note 1: Marriage record found in Greenfield Library, 10-7-95
Note 2: Living in Fry, Montana, in 1923, per Jacob estate.
Note 3: From Marcella Mickel: Rock Island, 14 March 1865: "a little daughter of Mrs. KINNICK, living about 6 miles above Sheffield in Bureau County, died in a fire last Thursday aged about 5 y. She was alone in the home at the time with another child, aged 18m. Mr. Kinnick is a soldier." This appears to be Amanda who died, the younger sister is Margaret. Joseph was mustered out of the Civil War service in St. Louis on 10 March 1865.
Note 4: 1900 census for son, Mark Edick, age 12, with father, William H., says divorced, living with his mother, Rachel A. Edick (found her after reading Joseph Kinnick pension file.
Note 5: Death year and place Per Rebecca Fraas, email Nov 1999.(had Mill Creek)
Note 6: Death date and county, per Montana Death Index, 1907-2002, ancestry.com

William H. (Bill) EDICK and Margaret Susana (Maggie) KINNICK had the following children:

+19	i.	**Helen EDICK**, born in Aug 1882, Iowa; married Jesse W. NELSON, in 1905.
20	ii.	**Clarence J. EDICK** was born in Nov 1884 in Iowa. Helen Edick search Note 1: 1900 census, Wyoming, Big Horn County, Cody, p. 13B, dwelling 304, family 309 has Margaret Edick, Jan 1863, 37, D, 3,3, IL, OH, OH, Hotel Keeper, with Daughter, Helen E. Aug 1882, 17, S, IA, IL, IL, At School; Son, Clarence J., Nov 1884, 15, S, same Son, Mark, Jan 1888, 12, S, Montana, IL, IL, At School
+21	iii.	**Mark EDICK**, born on 14 Jan 1886, Clyde Park, Park Co, Montana; died on 23 Jun 1970, Chehalis Hosp, Chehalis, Lewis Co, Washington.

12. **Tessa STOREY** (Elizabeth SCHWYHART-2, John-1) was born on 14 Oct 1871 in Kewanee, Henry Co, Illinois. She died on 3 Apr 1952 in Kewanee, Henry Co, Illinois. She was buried in Kewanee, Henry Co, Illinois.
Note 1: Per Judith K. Vermilion, 11 Oct 1998: All

Tessa STOREY and Frederick Arrored REILLY were married on 1 May 1906 in Kewanee, Henry Co, Illinois.

Frederick Arrored REILLY was born on 14 Oct 1869 in Mt. Pleasant, Henry Co, Iowa. He died on 7 Nov 1941 in Kewanee, Henry Co, Illinois. He was buried on 10 Nov 1941 in Kewanee, Henry Co, Illinois.
Note 1: Per Judith K. Vermilion, 11 Oct 1998: All

Tessa STOREY and Frederick Arrored REILLY had the following children:

+22	i.	**Lawrence Nestor REILLY**, born on 26 Feb 1909, Kewanee, Henry Co, Illinois; married Vivian Beatrice HOLLEY, on 12 Nov 1937, Chicago, Cook Co, Illinois; died on 14 Feb 1996, Cottonwood, Arizona.
+23	ii.	**Clarence Arrored REILLY**, born on 26 Feb 1909, Kewanee, Henry Co, Illinois; married Velma Hermina HEINRICK, on 5 May 1935, Kewanee, Henry Co, Illinois.
+24	iii.	**Edith Genevieve REILLY**, born on 23 Aug 1912, Kewanee, Henry Co, Illinois; married John Harvey KOMP, on 16 Mar 1937, Kewanee, Henry Co, Illinois; died on 5 Nov 1975, Kewanee, Henry Co, Illinois.

14. **Rosetta VAN_AKEN** (Susan SCHWYHART-2, John-1) was born on 26 Oct 1870 in Iowa. She died on 8 Jul 1955 in Hillsboro, Washington Co, Oregon.
Note 1: Per Rebecca Fraas, Nov 1999 email.
1880 Soundex, IA, Rosetta, 10, IA
Note 1: Tess has birth day, death info and marriage surname
Note 2: Linda has Rosetta, not Rose, also.

Rosetta VAN_AKEN and Niels Christian NIELSON were married.

Niels Christian NIELSON – more information sought.

Note 1: Sharon Barnes Jan 2009 email info.

Rosetta VAN_AKEN and Niels Christian NIELSON had the following children:

+25   i.   **James "Bill" NIELSON**, married Unknown UNKNOWN
           Note 1: Sharon Barnes Jan 2009 email info.

15. **LuLu Mae VAN_AKEN** (Susan SCHWYHART-2, John-1) was born in 1873 in Iowa. She died in Portland, Multnomah Co, Oregon.
Note 1: Per Rebecca Fraas, Nov 1999 email.
Note 2: 1880 Soundex, with parents, L. M., age 7, IA

LuLu Mae VAN_AKEN and August W. WURL were married in 1892.

August W. WURL was born in 1861 in New York.
Note 1: Per Rebecca Fraas, Nov 1999 email.
Note 2: 1910 census (26 Apr), 428 South K St, Livingston (City), Park Co, MT, has: August W. Wurl, 49, M1 18, NY, Ger, Ger, Carpenter, Railroad, with wife, Lulu M., 36, M1 18, 4, 4, IA, NY, OH; with four children listed (all 4 had parents, NY, IA): Minnie S., 16, NE (working as Servant, Private Home), Lillie M, 14, NE, Willie A., 12, NE, Carl O., 1 3/12, MT.
Note 3: 1920 census (5 Jan), Portland (city), 198 1/2 precinct, Multnomah Co, Oregon, 59 E. 52nd St., has three housing units, all family: 1) August Wurl, 57, NY, Ger2, fireman, hot house; with wife, Lue, 46, IA, NY, OH, and son, Carl, 10, MT, NY, IA. 2) Leon Kupp, 33, PA, US2, Stationary Engineer, Construction Company, with wife, Minnie, 26, NE, NY, IA, Check filer, Retail store, and his son, Raymond, 9, PA, PA, Eng, and his step-daughter (her daughter), Jeanette Moyer, 3, OR, MI, NE; 3) Arthur T. Bliss, 38, MT, WI, IL, Plumber, Plumbing Shop, with wife, Tillie, 24, NE, NY, IA, and twin sons, Chester and Raymond, 5, NE, MT, NE, and daughters: Beatrice, 4 10/12, and Juanita, 3 4/12, both also NE, MT, NE.
Note 4: 1930 census (same house address), has: August W. Wurl, O 3000, 66, Mat 31, NY, Ger2, Carpenter, Furniture Factory, with wife, Lue M., 55 Mat19, IA, NY, IL; and Susie Van Aken, mother-in-law, 76, M, IL, OH2, and a lodger/boarder: Robert Searl, 51, Eng3, Carpenter, Auto Garage.

LuLu Mae VAN_AKEN and August W. WURL had the following children:

+26   i.   **Minnie Susan WURL**, born in 1894, Nebraska.
+27   ii.   **Tillie Maud WURL**, born in 1896, Nebraska.
+28   iii.   **William Adelbert WURL**, born on 27 Apr 1898, Nebraska; married May UNKNOWN, in 1919; died in Jan 1985, Pomona, Los Angeles, CA.
29   iv.   **Carl Oliver WURL** was born on 17 Jan 1909 in Montana. He died in Sep 1976 in Portland, Multnomah Co, Oregon.
           Note 1: Per Rebecca Fraas, Nov 1999 email.
           Note 2: SSDI has: Carl Wurl, b. 17 Jan 1909, d. Sep 1976, last res: 97233, Portland, Multnomah Co, Oregon (Issued OR).

17. **John Jay VAN_AKEN** (Susan SCHWYHART-2, John-1) was born on 16 Sep 1880 in Stuart, Guthrie Co, Iowa. He died on 8 Mar 1967 in Livingston, Park Co, Montana.

Note 1: Per Rebecca Fraas, Nov 1999 email.
Note 2: 1900 Soundex MT, with Rachel A. Edick family as nephew.
Note 3: 1920 Soundex, MT, Park Co, Livingston has: South "I" Street, #209; with family.
Note 4::Tess has birth date 16 Sept 1880 rather than Aug 1880, plus additional details on death and marriage

John Jay VAN_AKEN and Ollie Esther WILLIAMS were married.

Ollie Esther WILLIAMS (daughter of Alvin WILLIAMS and Nancy Ann HONE) was born on 18 May 1889 in Illinois. She died on 12 Aug 1962 in Livingston, Park Co, Montana.
Note 1: 1920 Soundex, MT, see John, husband.
Note 2: Tess has 18 May 1889, IL (rather than 1890 Montana)

John Jay VAN_AKEN and Ollie Esther WILLIAMS had the following children:

+30　　　　　 i. **Pansy Naomi VANAKEN**, born on 4 Apr 1907, Livingston, Park Co, Montana; died on 10 Sep 1979, Missoula, Missoula Co, Montana.

+31　　　　　 ii. **Iva May VANAKEN**, born on 31 May 1912, Clyde Park, Park Co, Montana; married Russell H. (Pete) PERRY , Jr., on 14 Dec 1929, Amsterdam, Gallatin Co, Montana; died on 7 Feb 2001, Hamilton, Ravalli Co, Montana.

+32　　　　　 iii. **Vincent Vilroy VANAKEN**, born on 27 Oct 1915, Shields River, Gallain Co, Montana; married Altha Bernice COWAN, on 28 May 1939, Hamilton, Ravalli Co, Montana.

18. **Frank Adelbert VAN_AKEN** (Susan SCHWYHART-2, John-1) was born on 13 Nov 1893 in Nebraska. He died on 11 Feb 1970 in Forest Grove, Washington Co, Oregon.
Note 1: Per Rebecca Fraas, Nov 1999 email.
Note 2: Tess had birth and death information, marriage name

Frank Adelbert VAN_AKEN married Catherine Ella NARUP.

Catherine Ella NARUP - no further information available.

Chapter 5

Catherine SCHWYHART and Her Descendants

First Generation

1. **Catherine SCHWYHART** was born about 1819/20. She died about 1875.
Note 1: Per Folkert ancestor chart #99, Guernsey Co, OH

Catherine SCHWYHART and John LEWIS were married in 1840.

John LEWIS was born in 1817. He died in 1852 in Newcomerstown, Ohio.

Catherine SCHWYHART and John LEWIS had the following children:

+2   i.   **Sarah E. LEWIS**, born on 1 Nov 1843, Guernsey Co, Ohio; died on 10 Jul 1917, Guernsey Co, Ohio.

+3   ii.   **William Anderson LEWIS**, born on 18 Aug 1848; married Mary Jane SCHWYHART, on 3 May 1875; died on 22 Feb 1900.
Note 1: Information from Sandi Share, Mar 2006

Second Generation

2. **Sarah E. LEWIS** (Catherine SCHWYHART-1) was born on 1 Nov 1843 in Guernsey Co, Ohio. She died on 10 Jul 1917 in Guernsey Co, Ohio.

John FOLKERT was born on 5 Jun 1840 in Guernsey Co, Ohio. He died on 8 Mar 1913 in Guernsey Co, Ohio. Sarah E. LEWIS and John FOLKERT had the following children:

4   i.   **William D. FOLKERT** was born on 24 Mar 1914 in Guernsey Co, Ohio. He died on 26 Dec 1994 in Cambridge, Guernsey Co, Ohio.
SSDI has Wiliam D. Folkert, b. 24 Mar 1914, d. 26 Dec 1994, last res 43725, Cambridge, Guernsey CO, OH. (issued OH)

3. **William Anderson LEWIS** (Catherine SCHWYHART-1) was born on 18 Aug 1848. He died on 22 Feb 1900.
Note 1: Information from Sandi Share, Mar 2006

William Anderson LEWIS and Mary Jane SCHWYHART were married on 3 May 1875. **Mary Jane SCHWYHART** (daughter of Jacob SCHWYHART and Nancy DUFFEY) was born on 18 Dec 1848 in Ohio. She died in 1929.
Note 1: Information from Sandi Share, Mar 2006

1860 census, with family, only one.
Sharon has: Mary Jane (Lewis), b. 1848 (obit says 18 Dec)

Sandi Share, Mar 2006, info has Mary Jane as well... will use that, since strong family information source. William Anderson LEWIS and Mary Jane SCHWYHART had the following children:

5	i.	**Ida May LEWIS** was born in 1876 in Ohio.
		Note 1: Information from Sandi Share, Mar 2006
		Note 2: 1880 U.S. census
+6	ii.	**Jennie LEWIS**, born in Nov 1878, Ohio.
		Note 1: 1900 census
7	iii.	**Lillis LEWIS** was born in Nov 1880 in Ohio.
		Note 1: Information from Sandi Share, Mar 2006
		Note 2: 1900 census
+8	iv.	**Wilma Sue LEWIS**, born in Jan 1884, Ohio; married Philip Christopher WEARSCH, in 1903.
		Note 1: 1900 U.S. census
		Note 2: 1910 U.S. census

Third Generation

6. **Jennie LEWIS** (William Anderson-2, Catherine SCHWYHART-1) was born in Nov 1878 in Ohio.
Note 1: 1900 U.S. census
Jacob WEARSCH was born in 1878 in Ohio.
Note 1: 1920 U.S. census

Jennie LEWIS and Jacob WEARSCH had the following children:

9	i.	**Lewis WEARSCH** was born in 1905 in Ohio.
		Note 1: 1920 U.S. census

8. **Wilma Sue LEWIS** (William Anderson-2, Catherine SCHWYHART-1) was born in Jan 1884 in Ohio.
Note 1: Information from Sandi Share, Mar 2006
Note 2: 1900 U.S. Census
Note 3: Philip Wearsch found in:U.S. Atlantic and Great Lakes - Census Index (1880):
   State: Ohio
   County: Lorain
   Township: Avon
   Relationship to Head: Son
   Age: 6
   Gender: Male

Race: White
Marital Status: Single
Birthplace: OHIO
Birth Year: <1874>
Mother Birthplace: BAVARIA
Father Birthplace: PRUSSIA
Roll: T9_1042
Page: 337D
ED: 162   [from Genealogy.com]

Wilma Sue LEWIS and Philip Christopher WEARSCH were married in 1903. (1910 U.S. census)

Philip Christopher WEARSCH was born in 1874 in Ohio. He died in 1956. Philip Wearsch found in:
U.S. Atlantic and Great Lakes - Census Index (1880)
State: Ohio
County: Lorain
Township: Avon
Relationship to Head: Son
Age: 6
Gender: Male
Race: White
Marital Status: Single
Birthplace: OHIO
Birth Year: <1874>
Mother Birthplace: BAVARIA
Father Birthplace: PRUSSIA
Roll: T9_1042
Page: 337D
ED: 162   [from Genealogy.com]

Wilma Sue LEWIS and Philip Christopher WEARSCH had the following children:

10	i.	**Mary Elizabeth WEARSCH** was born in 1904 in Ohio. She died in 1983. Note 1: 1910 U.S. census
+11	ii.	**Charles Gordon WEARSCH**, born in 1906, Ohio; married Barbara I. HUTTON, in 1927; died in Jul 1977. Note 1: 1930 U.S. census
12	iii.	**Lillis Ruth WEARSCH** was born in 1908 in Ohio. Note 1: 1910 U.S. census
13	iv.	**Robert Lewis WEARSCH** was born on 27 Apr 1910 in Ohio. He died on 17 Feb 1988. Note 1: Information from Sandi Share, Mar 2006 Note 2: From Ancestry.com, 26 Apr 2005
+14	v.	**Doris WEARSCH**, born in 1914.
15	vi.	**Walter Hayes WEARSCH** was born in 1917 in Ohio.

Note 1: Information from Sandi Share, Mar 2006
Note 2: 1930 U.S. census

Chapter 7

Joseph Z. SCHWYHART and His Descendants

First Generation

1. **Joseph Z. Jr. SCHWYHART** was born in Sep 1822 in Guernsey Co, Ohio. He died on 21 May 1905 in Knox Twp, Guernsey Co, Ohio. He was buried in Birds Run Cemetery, Knox Twp, Guernsey Co, Ohio.

Note 1: Per Knox Township, Guernsey Co, OH records; had birth year about 1811.

Note 2: Guernsey Co, OH: 1900 federal census, Knox Twp, has Sep 1822, age 77. Married 50 years, 1850.

Note 3: Wheeling Twp, 1860 had 33, should be 37 per 1900 birth date.

Note 4: Wheeling Twp, 1870 had 48, should be 47 per 1900 birth date.

Note 5: Knox Twp, 1880 had 60, should be 57 per 1900 birth date.

Note 6: Not found in 1910 census, assume died in between.

Note 7: Per Karen Nucci, Aug 1999: Has 29 May, not Sep 1822; d. 31 May 1905 (I had 1900/10 est), Knox twp, Guernsey Co, Birds Run Cemetery

Note 8: After marriage, lived in Wheeling Township, Guernsey Co for sixteen years, moved to Knox township thereafter; had 11 children, eight living (listed).

Note 9: 1880 census, Knox Twp, Guernsey Co, OH, has: Joseph, 60, farming, Rachel, 50, James M., 27, Sarah, 23, Martha, 21, Jane, 17, Eliza, 14, Annie, 13, Cordia, 9. Children not there: Maria (married, I assume), John, and Hattie. Annie is Barbara Ann, Mary Jane goes by Jane.

Note 10: Pension file has 3 boys and 8 girls for children - missing a boy, deceased by Jun 1898.

Joseph Z. Jr. SCHWYHART and Rachel Anne MERCER were married on 15 Jan 1850 in Wheeling Twp, Guernsey Co, Ohio.

Rachel Anne MERCER (daughter of James MERCER and Maria UNKNOWN) was born in Sep 1830 in Ohio. She died between 1900 and 1910.

Note 1: Per Knox Township, Guernsey Co, OH records

Note 2: Guernsey Co, OH: 1900 federal census, Knox Twp, has Sep 1830, age 69. Married 50 years, 1850. Wheeling Twp, 1860 had 29, should be 29 per 1900 birth date. Wheeling Twp, 1870 had 43, should be 39 per 1900 birth date. Knox Twp, 1880 had 50, should be 49 per 1900 birth date. Not found in 1910 census, assume died in between.

Note 1: Marriage details from Pension file.

Joseph Z. Jr. SCHWYHART and Rachel Anne MERCER had the following children:

| +2 | i. | **Maria Elizabeth SCHWYHART**, born on 23 Jan 1851, Ohio. |
| 3 | ii. | **James Mercer SCHWYHART** was born on 18 Nov 1852 in Ohio. He died after 1930. |

3 ii. **James Mercer SCHWYHART** was born on 18 Nov 1852 in Ohio. He died after 1930.
Note 1: Federal census, Nov 1853, OH, per 1900; 1860, 7, 1870, 18, 1880, 27, 1900, 46, with family; 1910, 56, 1920, 62!, with sister, Eliza.

Note 2: 1910 census, Ohio, Guernsey Co, Know twp, Music Teacher, Public School, 56, in household with sister, Eliza, 43, and a boarder, another school teacher, 20.

Note 3: 1930 census, Knox Two, Guernsey Co, OH, has: James M., 77, and Eliza, Sister, 63.

Note 4: Middle name and birth date from Pension File of father.

4   iii. **Sarah E. SCHWYHART** was born in 1856. She died before Jun 1898.

Note 1: Listed in 1870 census, with rest of family.

Note 2: Death estimate from father's Pension File

+5   iv. **Martha S. SCHWYHART**, born in 1858, Ohio; married William J. POLLOCK, in 1897; died before Jun 1898.

6   v. **John SCHWYHART** was born in 1859 in Ohio. He died before Jun 1898.

Note 1: John appears in 1860 census as age 8/12 - does not appear again....

Note 2: Is not in 1880 census, gone on in life, or deceased??

Note 3: Estimated death date based on father's Pension File information

+7   vi. **Mary Jane SCHWYHART**, born on 30 Oct 1861, Ohio.

8   vii. **Eliza SCHWYHART** was born on 7 Jul 1865 in Ohio.

Note 1: Federal census, Jul 1865, OH, per 1900; 1870, 6, 1880, 14, 1900, 34, with family; 1910, 43, 1920, 52, with brother, James M.

Note 2: Day of birth, from father's Pension File.

9   viii. **Barbara Ann SCHWYHART** was born on 13 Jul 1867 in Ohio.

Note 1: Federal census, 1870, 4, 1880, 13, 1900, (Anna B.) 34, with family.

Note 2: 1910, 38, with Pollock family, Dressmaker.

Note 3: Ohio Deaths, 1958-2000, has a Barbara A. Schwyhart, died 6 Apr 1958.

Note 4: Birth day from father's Pension File.

+10   ix. **Hattie Mae SCHWYHART**, born in 1869, Ohio; married Harvey Day TEBOW, Kansas; died on 4 Oct 1922, Jamestown, Cloud Co, Kansas.

Note 1: Patricia Tebow Williams, Jun 2006 email.

+11   x. **Corda Belle SCHWYHART**, born on 18 Nov 1871, Ohio; died on 24 Oct 1962, Cambridge, Guernsey Co, Ohio.

Second Generation

2. **Maria Elizabeth SCHWYHART** (Joseph Z. Jr.-1) was born on 23 Jan 1851 in Ohio.

Note 1: Federal census, 1860, 9, 1870, 19, with family.

Note 2: 1870, 29, with husband, John Dawson.

Note 3: Full name and birth date from Pension File.

Maria Elizabeth SCHWYHART married John T. DAWSON – details pending.

John T. DAWSON was born in 1841 in Ohio.

Note 1: 1880 census, John L. Dawson, 39, OH, Farmer (prior note) - look at actual:

Note 2: John T. Dawson, 32, Liberty Twp, Guernsey Co, OH, with Maria E., 28, James T. , 7, and Annie S., 1, with sister-in-law, Martha S., 22, servant.

Maria Elizabeth SCHWYHART and John T. DAWSON had the following children:

> 12   i. **James T. SCHWYHART** was born in 1873 in Ohio.
>   Liberty Twp, Guernsey Co, OH, census of 1880: 7, OH
>
> 13   ii. **Annie S. SCHWYHART** was born in 1879 in Ohio.
>   Liberty Twp, Guernsey Co, OH, census of 1880: 1, OH

5. **Martha S. SCHWYHART** (Joseph Z. Jr.-1) was born in 1858 in Ohio. She died before Jun 1898.
Note 1: Federal census, 1860, 3, 1870, 12, 1880, 21, with family; 1910, 43, with husband, William J. Pollock; 1920, 53.
Note 2: Seems to appear twice in 1880 census, once with her parents, and again with her older sister, Maria and her husband, John L Duncan.

Martha S. SCHWYHART and William J. POLLOCK were married in 1897.

William J. POLLOCK was born in 1869 in Ohio.
Note 1: 1910 and 1920 census, wife of Mamie J., 41 & 51, OH, father born in Ireland, mother in OH. Blacksmith both, own shop. One son listed both. Only child per 1910 census, married 13 years.
Note 2: Assume Martha had died, and Mamie is new wife, mother of Charles. - Per anaylys of Joseph Pension File.

Martha S. SCHWYHART and William J. POLLOCK had the following children:

> 14   i. **Charles E. POLLOCK** was born in 1902 in Ohio.
>   Note 1: 1910 and 1920 census, 8 and 18, Teacher in Com School in latter.

7. **Mary Jane SCHWYHART** (Joseph Z. Jr.-1) was born on 30 Oct 1861 in Ohio.
Note 1: Federal census, 1870, 9, 1880, 17, with family.
Note 2: Birth date from father's Pension File.

Mary Jane SCHWYHART and William A. LEWIS married – details sought.

William A. LEWIS was born in 1846 in Wheeling Twp, Guernsey Co, Ohio.
Note 1: Per Guernsey Co profile of son.

Mary Jane SCHWYHART and William A. LEWIS had the following children:

> 15   i. **Ida LEWIS**
> 16   ii. **Lillis LEWIS** was born in Nov 1880 in Ohio.
>   Note 1: Sandi Share, Mar 2006
>   Note 2: 1900 U. S. census
> +17   iii. **Jennie LEWIS**, born in Nov 1878, Ohio
>   Note 1: 1900 U. S. census
> +18   iv. **Wilma LEWIS**, married Philip WEARSCH, in 1903.

10. **Hattie Mae SCHWYHART** (Joseph Z. Jr.-1) was born in 1869 in Ohio. She died on 4 Oct 1922 in Jamestown, Cloud Co, Kansas. She was buried in Jamestown, Cloud Co, Kansas.
Note 1: 1870 census has Hattie Mae as age 1.
Note 2: Not listed in 1880 with the family.
Note 3: Patricia Tebow Williams, Jun 2006 email.

Hattie Mae SCHWYHART and Harvey Day TEBOW were married in Kansas.
Note 1: Patricia Tebow Williams, Jun 2006 email.

Harvey Day TEBOW – additional details sought.
Note 1: Patricia Tebow Williams, Jun 2006 email.

Hattie Mae SCHWYHART and Harvey Day TEBOW had the following children:

19	i.	**Alfred Edward TEBOW** was born on 26 Oct 1885 in Kansas. He died in Nov 1971.	

Note 1: Patricia Tebow Williams, Jun 2006 email.

20 ii. **Louis Walter TEBOW** was born on 22 Feb 1887 in Kansas.
Note 1: Patricia Tebow Williams, Jun 2006 email.

+21 iii. **Harvey Day TEBOW Jr.**, born on 26 Aug 1889, Jamestown, Cloud Co, Kansas; married Julia Elliott SEE, on 27 May 1918, Concordia, Cloud Co, Kansas; died on 21 Jul 1947, Peoria, IL.
Note 1: Patricia Tebow Williams, Jun 2006 email.

22 iv. **Eugene Field TEBOW** was born on 27 Jan 1896 in Kansas. He died on 14 Feb 1978 in Santa Barbara, California.
Note 1: Patricia Tebow Williams, Jun 2006 email.

11. **Corda Belle SCHWYHART** (Joseph Z. Jr.-1) was born on 18 Nov 1871 in Ohio. She died on 24 Oct 1962 in Cambridge, Guernsey Co, Ohio.
Note 1: Federal census, 1880, 9, with family.
Note 2: Full birth date, and correct spelling of name, Corda Belle, from father's Pension File. Ohio Deaths, 1958-2000, has Corda B. Nelson, d. 24 Oct 1962, Widowed, 90, Cambridge, Guernsey Co, Ohio.
Note 3: 1920 census for Know Twp, Guernsey Co, OH, has: Corda B. Nelson, 48, wd, OH3, farmer, with daughter, Eva M., 10, OH3, and mother-in-law, Ester, 83, wd, Oh, Ire, Va.

John NELSON died before 1920. Corda Belle SCHWYHART and John NELSON had the following children:

+23 i. **Eva Mae NELSON**, born in 1910, Ohio.

Third Generation

17. **Jennie LEWIS** (Mary Jane SCHWYHART-2, Joseph Z. Jr.-1) was born in Nov 1878 in

Ohio.
Note 1: 1900 U. S. census

Jennie LEWIS and Jacob WEARSCH were married – details sought.

Jacob WEARSCH was born in 1878 in Ohio.
Note 1: 1920 U. S. census

Jennie LEWIS and Jacob WEARSCH had the following children:

24	i.	**Lewis WEARSCH** was born in 1905 in Ohio.
		Note 1: 1920 U. S. census

18. **Wilma LEWIS** (Mary Jane SCHWYHART-2, Joseph Z. Jr.-1)

Wilma LEWIS and Philip WEARSCH were married in 1903. **Philip WEARSCH** was born.
Wilma LEWIS and Philip WEARSCH had the following children:

+25	i.	**Mary WEARSCH**, born in 1904.
26	ii.	**Gordon WEARSCH** was born in 1906. He died in 1977 in Guernsey Co, Ohio.
27	iii.	**Ruth WEARSCH** was born in 1909. She died in 1917.
28	iv.	**Robert WEARSCH** was born in 1912.
+29	v.	**Doris WEARSCH**, born in 1914.
30	vi.	**Hayes WEARSCH** was born in 1916.

21. **Harvey Day TEBOW Jr.** (Hattie Mae SCHWYHART-2, Joseph Z. Jr.-1) was born on 26 Aug 1889 in Jamestown, Cloud Co, Kansas. He died on 21 Jul 1947 in Peoria, IL.
Note 1: Patricia Tebow Williams, Jun 2006 email.

Harvey Day TEBOW Jr. and Julia Elliott SEE were married on 27 May 1918 in Concordia, Cloud Co, Kansas.
Note 1: Patricia Tebow Williams, Jun 2006 email.

Julia Elliott SEE – details sought.
Note 1: Patricia Tebow Williams, Jun 2006 email.

23. **Eva Mae NELSON** (Corda Belle SCHWYHART-2, Joseph Z. Jr.-1) was born in 1910 in Ohio.

Eva Mae Nelson married Unknown BAIRD – additional information sought.

Unknown BAIRD – details sought.

Chapter 7

Jacob SCHWYHART and His Descendants

First Generation

1. **Jacob SCHWYHART** was born on 6 Aug 1826 in Belmont Co, Ohio. He died on 25 Aug 1885 in Wheeling Twp, Guernsey Co, Ohio.
Note 1: Wheeling Twp, Guernsey Co, OH: Jacob, 34, 54, OH, in 1860 and 1880 Federal census - Farmer.
Note 2: Per Karen Nucci, Aug 1999: Birth and death dates and places

Jacob SCHWYHART and Nancy DUFFEY were married on 20 Apr 1848.

Nancy DUFFEY was born in 1827 in Ohio. She died on 20 Jan 1920.
Note 1: 1860 and 1880 census with husband, Jacob, and family, 33 and 53. 1900 census with son, I.N., age 74; 1920 census, 93, widowed, with Isaac.

Jacob SCHWYHART and Nancy DUFFEY had the following children:

+2	i.	**Mary Jane SCHWYHART**, born on 18 Dec 1848, Ohio; married William Anderson LEWIS, on 3 May 1875; died in 1929. Note 1: Sandi Share, Mar 2006.
+3	ii.	**William A. SCHWYHART**, born in May 1850, Ohio; married Eliza Jane (Jennie) UNKNOWN, in 1878.
+4	iii.	**John C. SCHWYHART**, born in Sep 1851, Ohio; married Olive B. NORTH, in 1885.
+5	iv.	**Isaac N. SCHWYHART**, born in Jul 1855, Ohio; married Martha GIBSON, on 10 Aug 1910.
+6	v.	**Joseph Thomas SCHWYHART**, born on 24 Aug 1856, Ohio; married Mary Elizabeth MARLING, on 22 Apr 1879; died on 5 Jun 1936.
+7	vi.	**Martha S. SCHWYHART**, born in 1858, Ohio.
+8	vii.	**Emma SCHWYHART**, born in Aug 1860, Ohio; died on 22 Feb 1935.
9	viii.	**Jacob James SCHWYHART** was born on 21 Oct 1862 in Ohio. He died on 23 Aug 1886. Note 1: Wheeling Twp, Guernsey Co, OH: Jacob, 17, in 1880 Federal census Note 1: Sharon has Jacob James, b. 21 Oct 1862, d. 23 Aug 1886
10	ix.	**Ida Mae SCHWYHART** was born on 10 Apr 1865 in Ohio. She died on 12 Dec 1888. Note 1: Wheeling Twp, Guernsey Co, OH: Ida 15, in 1880 Federal census only Note 2: Sharon has: Ida Mae, b. 10 Apr 1865, d. 12 Dec 1888
+11	x.	**Lemuel G. SCHWYHART**, born on 20 Jun 1869, Ohio; married Martha

GIBSON, on 31 Dec 1891; died in 1901.

Second Generation

2. **Mary Jane SCHWYHART** (Jacob-1) was born on 18 Dec 1848 in Ohio. She died in 1929.
Note 1: 1860 census, with family, only one.
Note 2: Sharon has: Mary Jane (Lewis), b. 1848 (obit says 18 Dec)
Note 3: Sandi Share, Mar 2006, info has Mary Jane as well... will use that, since strong family information source.

Mary Jane SCHWYHART and William Anderson LEWIS were married on 3 May 1875.

William Anderson LEWIS (son of John LEWIS and Catherine SCHWYHART) was born on 18 Aug 1848. He died on 22 Feb 1900.
Note 1: Sandi Share, Mar 2006.

Mary Jane SCHWYHART and William Anderson LEWIS had the following children:

12	i.	**Ida May LEWIS** was born in 1876 in Ohio.
		Note 1: Sandi Share, Mar 2006.
		Note 2: 1880 U. S. census
+13	ii.	**Jennie LEWIS**, born in Nov 1878, Ohio.
		Note 1: 1900 U. S. census
14	iii.	**Lillis LEWIS** was born in Nov 1880 in Ohio.
		Note 1: Sandi Share, Mar 2006.
		Note 2: 1900 census
+15	iv.	**Wilma Sue LEWIS**, born in Jan 1884, Ohio; married Philip Christopher WEARSCH, in 1903
		Note 1: 1900 U. S. census
		Note 2: 1910 U. S. census

3. **William A. SCHWYHART** (Jacob-1) was born in May 1850 in Ohio.
Note 1: 1860 and 1880 census, 10 & 30 1900 census, May 1850, OH, wife, Jane, married 22, 9-8 ch 1920 census, Wheeling Twp, Guernsey Co, OH, age 64, initial, A., wife, Eliza. He was listed a Will A. in 1920.
Note 2: 1910 census Guernsey Co, Wheeling Twp, has William A, 59, M1 34 OH3, Farmer, w/wife, Jennie, 53, M1 34 10 8 OH3 with son Willa M., 13, OH3 and daughter, Lestie, daughter, 18 S, OH3, Servant, House Keeper.
Note 3: 1920 census, has Will A. Schwjhard and Eliza J, in Wheeling, Guernsey, Ohio, b. about 1851

William A. SCHWYHART and Eliza Jane (Jennie) UNKNOWN were married in 1878.

Eliza Jane (Jennie) UNKNOWN was born in Jul 1859 in Ohio.
Note 1: Wheeling Twp, Guernsey Co, OH: Jane in 1880, 1900: 22, 41; 1920, 62, as Eliza J. 1900

says m 22, 9-8. Didn't find family in 1910 (did, later, see Husband). Appears in 1880 census, that Eliza Jane was married before, as there were Jane Atkins, 5, listed as step-daughter, and Virgil Atkins, 2, listed in the household; along with J. or Z. Schwyhart, son, age 5/12 born in Jan. Are missing three children, probably born, based on years, between each of last four!

William A. SCHWYHART and Eliza Jane (Jennie) UNKNOWN had the following children:

16	i.	**J. Z. SCHWYHART** was born in Jan 1879 in Ohio. Note 1: Wheeling Twp, Guernsey Co, OH: 1880 census, born in Jan, age 5/12
17	ii.	**Walter S. SCHWYHART** was born in Jul 1880 in Ohio. Note 1: Wheeling Twp, Guernsey Co, OH: 1900, 19, with birth date and state
+18	iii.	**Charles H. SCHWYHART**, born in Nov 1882, Ohio.
19	iv.	**Mary A. SCHWYHART** was born in Apr 1887 in Ohio. Note 1: Wheeling Twp, Guernsey Co, OH: 1900, 13, with birth date and state
+20	v.	**Luella (Lestie)(Lesta) SCHWYHART**, born in Feb 1892, Kimbolton, Ohio; married J. Carl MCCLAUGHRY, Guernsey Cemetery, Guernsey Co, Ohio; died on 16 Nov 1989, St. Petersburg, Pinella County, Florida.
21	vi.	**Willie (Willa M.) SCHWYHART** was born in Jan 1897 in Ohio. Wheeling Twp, Guernsey Co, OH: 1900, 3, with birth date and state Note 1: Listed with parents in 1910 as son, Willa M., 13.

4. **John C. SCHWYHART** (Jacob-1) was born in Sep 1851 in Ohio.
Note 1: Wheeling Twp, Guernsey Co, OH: John, 9, 28, in 1860 and 1880 Federal census Sep 1851, OH; 48, 58, 68, in 1900, 1910, 1920, Belle Plaine Twp, Sumner Co, KS - Farmer.
Note 2: 1930 census for Belle Plaine, Sumner Co, KS, has: John C., 78, b. 1851, OH, with wife, O. Beulah, 60, 1869, and two: son, Wilbur g. 27, 1902, and granddaughter, Bula M. Schwyhart, 19, 1914.
Note 3: In 1883 John and his brother "Ike" came west to Kansas "to seek their fortune." The remainder of his family was very much afraid for them because of the Indians in Kansas.
Doug Carr Packet, July 2008

John C. SCHWYHART and Olive B. NORTH were married in 1885.

Olive B. NORTH (daughter of William Henry Harrison "Tip" NORTH and Catherine (Kate) FULLER) was born in Nov 1868 in Iowa.
Note 1: Federal census 1900, 1910, 1920 has her 31, 41, 50; 1910 has m1 25 8-8, all listed! Her father (Harrison North in 1900! under Schuyhart in gen.com) on 1900, 1910, not 1920.

John C. SCHWYHART and Olive B. NORTH had the following children:

+22	i.	**Mossie A. (Mossagate) SCHWYHART**, born in Jun 1886, Kansas; married Chester Arthur MASON.
+23	ii.	**Harrison Earl SCHWYHART**, born on 11 Jul 1890, Oklahoma; married Alice Fae WHITNEY; married Veva Venita BEAVER, in 1925; died in Jun

1963, Kansas.

+24   iii.   **Paul Dewey SCHWYHART**, born on 24 Oct 1892, Oklahoma (Indian Territory).

+25   iv.   **Ida Marie SCHWYHART**, born on 21 Mar 1895, Kansas; married Arthur Gilbert HUNT.

Note 1: Doug Carr Schwyhart North packet, July 2008.

26   v.   **Calvin Newton SCHWYHART** was born on 30 May 1898 in Belle Plaine, Sumner Co, Kansas. He died a tragic death in an accident with a wagon and team of horses, at the age of 18 in 1916.

Note 1: Doug Carr Schwyhart North packet, July 2008.

Note 2: Federal census, Belle Plaine Twp, Sumner Co, Kansas for 1900, 1910, 1920, 3, 12, not listed. Middle initial either N. or M.

Note 3: He was dating Emma Stephenson at the time of his death, at age 18.

27   vi.   **Jay Wesley SCHWYHART** was born on 24 Mar 1900 in Belle Plaine, Sumner Co, Kansas. He died of a heart attack coming in from harvest field. in 1922.

Note 1: Federal census, Belle Plaine Twp, Sumner Co, Kansas for 1900, 1910, 1920, 2/12, 10, 19.

Note 2: "He was our schoolteacher of the family and he, too, suffered a tragic death from a heart attack while coming in from the harvest field. He was 22 years of age." "He was engaged to marry Olive Hatfield." Doug Carr Packet, July 2008

28   vii.   **Wilbur George SCHWYHART** was born on 29 Oct 1903 in Belle Plaine, Sumner Co, Kansas. He died in Dec 1978 in Mulvane, Sumner Co, KS.

Note 1: Federal census, Belle Plaine Twp, Sumner Co, Kansas for 1910, 1920, 5, 16.

Note 2: SSDI has Wilbur Schwyhart, b. 29 Oct 1903, d. Dec 1978, Mulvane, Sumner Co, KS (Issued KS)

Note 3: Doug Carr Schwyhart North packet, July 2008.

Note 4: Wilbur had no descendants, but his family remembers the care he provided in his mother's last years! Doug Carr Packet, July 2008

+29   viii.   **Helen Elnora SCHWYHART**, born on 23 Jun 1906, Belle Plaine, Sumner Co, Kansas; married Glen Elias CARR.

Note 1: Doug Carr Schwyhart North packet, July 2008.

30   ix.   **Bula M. SCHWYHART** was born in 1915 in Missouri.

Note 1: Federal census, Belle Plaine Twp, Sumner Co, Kansas for 1920, 5, born in Missouri, but, family in Kansas in both 1910 and 1920.

Note 2: Jul 2008 - not a daughter, per Doug Carr packet

5. Isaac N. SCHWYHART (Jacob-1) was born in Jul 1855 in Ohio.

Note 1: Wheeling Twp, Guernsey Co, OH: Isaac N., 6, 26, in 1860 and 1880 Federal census

Note 2: 1900 census, still there, 44, with wife, Martha, 42. Also there in 1920, age listed at 66. Appears that two oldest children listed, may be Martha's by a prior marriage, plus two of their own, perhaps.

Note 3: Guernsey Co Gen Soc, 10 Jun 1996 packet, Gibson Family Records, Martha Gibson #3504, married Lemuel and then I.N. Says children by Lemuel are Grace, Alta, Wilma; children my I.N. are Ruth, Child m. Charles Braniger, Faye.

Note 4: Putting these two together, Ada R. would be Ruth, Grace would be Child and Faye is a third, I think, and will assume, at this point (9-99).
Note 5: 1910 census, OH, Guernsey Co, Wheeling Twp, has: Isaac N. Schwyhart, Head, 56, S. OH3, Farmer, with Nancy Schwyhart, his mother, 83, Wd, 10 7, OH, Eng, Eng, Own Income, along with Martha Schwyhart, sister-in-law, 35, 3 2, Servant, Private Family, and 2 nieces, Gracie, 12, OH3, and Alta, 8, OH3.
Note 6: In 1883 John and his brother "Ike" came west to Kansas "to seek their fortune." The remainder of his family was very much afraid for them because of the Indians in Kansas.
Doug Carr Packet, July 2008

Isaac N. SCHWYHART and Martha GIBSON were married on 10 Aug 1910.

Martha GIBSON was born on 8 Aug 1873 in Liberty Twp, Guernsey Co, Ohio. She died in 1931 in Liberty Twp, Guernsey Co, Ohio. She was buried in Guernsey Cemetery, Guernsey Co, Ohio.
Note 1: Wheeling Twp, Guernsey Co, OH: 42 in 1920 Federal census.
Guernsey Co Gen Soc, 10 Jun 1996 packet, Gibson Family Records, Martha Gibson #3504, married Lemuel and then I.N.
Note 2: Sharon has d. 2 March 1932 rather than 1931.
Note 3: Sharon says: When Lem died in 1901, Martha moved in with Lem's parents, Jacob and Nancy. Word was sent to his brother, Isaac, who lived out west somewhere - maybe Indian Territory which later became Kansas, to come home to help take care of his brother's family. So he came back and in a few years, he married his brother's widow.

Isaac N. SCHWYHART and Martha GIBSON had the following children:

+31	i.	**Gladys SCHWYHART**, born on 31 May 1911, Ohio; married Charles BRANIGER, in Sep 1931; died on 31 Jan 1982.
32	ii.	**Ada R. SCHWYHART** was born on 14 Nov 1914 in Ohio. She died on 14 Oct 1984.
		Note 1: Wheeling Twp, Guernsey Co, OH: 1920, 5
		Note 2: Sharon has: Ada Ruth, b. 14 Nov 1914, d. 14 Oct 1984, unmarried.
		Note 3: SSDI has these dates for Ada, issues OH.
33	iii.	**Faye SCHWYHART** was born in 1917. She died in 1919.
		Note 1: Guernsey Co Gen Soc, 10 Jun 1996 packet, Gibson Family Records, Martha Gibson #3504, married Lemuel and then I.N. Says children by Lemuel are Grace, Alta, Wilma; children my I.N. are Ruth, Child m. Charles Braniger, Faye.
		Note 2: Sharon has: Faye, b. 1917 or 1918, d. a year or two later

6. **Joseph Thomas SCHWYHART** (Jacob-1) was born on 24 Aug 1856 in Ohio. He died on 5 Jun 1936. He was buried in Kimbolton Cemetery, OH.
Note 1: Wheeling Twp, Guernsey Co, OH: Joseph 4, 24, in 1860 and 1880 Federal census, with wife, Elizabeth, 21, and, daughter, Callie, 1, in 1880. 1900 census has the family in Liberty Twp, with four more children, he as 44, born Aug 1855, 54 in 1910 and 64 in 1920.
Note 2: Sharon has: Joseph T., b. 1855, (obit says b. 24 Aug 1856, d. 5 Jun 1936 - burns, oil lamp fire)

Note 3: Melba has birth date as 24 Aug 1856, not Aug 1855.
Note 4: Joseph died as a result of burns he suffered when an oil lamb overturned and caught his bedding on fire.

Joseph Thomas SCHWYHART and Mary Elizabeth MARLING were married on 22 Apr 1879.

Mary Elizabeth MARLING (daughter of Isaac Oldham MARLING and Martha BONNELL) was born on 7 Dec 1856 in Washington, Ohio. She died on 9 Sep 1920 in Ohio. She was buried in Kimbolton Cemetery, OH.
Note 1: Liberty Twp, Guernsey Co, OH: 1900, 1910, 1920 census, 43, 53, 63; married 1879, per 1900 census, 5-5.
Note 2: Last name from Melba.
Note 3: Wheeling Twp, Guernsey Co, OH: Joseph 4, 24, in 1860 and 1880 Federal census, with wife, Elizabeth, 21, and, daughter, Callie, 1, in 1880. Would appear Callie may have been a daughter from a prior marriage.
Note 4: Oldest daughter of the marriage is Eva Belle, born 26 Oct 1880.

Joseph Thomas SCHWYHART and Mary Elizabeth MARLING had the following children:

+34	i.	**Eva Belle SCHWYHART**, born on 26 Oct 1880; died on 9 Apr 1957.
+35	ii.	**Maud A. SCHWYHART**, born in Jun 1881, Ohio; died on 14 Jul 1969.
+36	iii.	**Naphtali (Naph) SCHWYHART**, born in Apr 1885, Ohio; married Lillian 'Mae' WILSON, in 1907; died on 22 Apr 1954.
+37	iv.	**Mary 'Bernice' SCHWYHART**, born on 5 Feb 1889, Ohio; died in Apr 1968.
+38	v.	**Joseph 'Ralph' SCHWYHART**, born on 29 May 1894, Liberty Twp, Guernsey Co, Ohio; married Lelia Kathryn KENNEDY, on 28 Jun 1916, Cambridge, Guernsey Co, Ohio; died on 18 Dec 1975, Guernsey Co, Ohio.

7. **Martha S. SCHWYHART** (Jacob-1) was born in 1858 in Ohio.
Wheeling Twp, Guernsey Co, OH: Martha S. in 1860 Federal census only.
Sharon has: Martha Susan (Dull), b. 1858 (obit said 28 Dec 1859)

Martha S. SCHWYHART married Unknown Dull – more information sought.

Unknown DULL – details sought.

8. **Emma SCHWYHART** (Jacob-1) was born in Aug 1860 in Ohio. She died on 22 Feb 1935.
Wheeling Twp, Guernsey Co, OH: Emma, 7/12 in 1860 Federal census 39 in 1900 with I.N.
Sharon has: d. 1935 or 36

Emma SCHWYHART married Unknown WOODARD – more information sought.

Unknown WOODARD – details sought

11. **Lemuel G. SCHWYHART** (Jacob-1) was born on 20 Jun 1869 in Ohio. He died in 1901. Wheeling Twp, Guernsey Co, OH:
Note 1: Lemuel, 13, in 1880 Federal census
Note 2: Guernsey Co Gen Soc, 10 Jun 1996 packet, Gibson Family Records, Martha Gibson #3504, married Lemuel and then I.N. (brothers): Lemuel G., d. 1901
Note 3: Sharon (descendant) has: Simon G. (known as Lem, Lemuel, or Lemmon), b. 20 June 1869, d. 1901 from an infected tooth

Lemuel G. SCHWYHART and Martha GIBSON were married on 31 Dec 1891.

Martha GIBSON was born on 8 Aug 1873 in Liberty Twp, Guernsey Co, Ohio. She died in 1931 in Liberty Twp, Guernsey Co, Ohio. She was buried in Guernsey Cem, Guernsey Co, Ohio.
Note 1: Wheeling Twp, Guernsey Co, OH: 42 in 1920 Federal census.
Note 2: Guernsey Co Gen Soc, 10 Jun 1996 packet, Gibson Family Records, Martha Gibson #3504, married Lemuel and then I.N.
Note 3: Sharon has d. 2 March 1932 rather than 1931.
Note 4: Sharon says: When Lem died in 1901, Martha moved in with Lem's parents, Jacob and Nancy. Word was sent to his brother, Isaac, who lived out west somewhere - maybe Indian Territory which later became Kansas, to come home to help take care of his brother's family. So he came back and in a few years, he married his brother's widow.

Lemuel G. SCHWYHART and Martha GIBSON had the following children:

+39   i.   **Lillis Grace SCHWYHART**, born on 13 May 1897; married Clarence Peiter HILL, on 12 Nov 1921; died on 4 Sep 1980.

40   ii.   **Mary Wilma SCHWYHART** was born on 22 May 1894. She died on 26 Jun 1896.
Note 1: Guernsey Co Gen Soc, 10 Jun 1996 packet, Gibson Family Records, Martha Gibson #3504, married Lemuel and then I.N. Says children by Lemuel are Grace, Alta, Wilma; children by I.N. are Ruth, Child m. Charles Braniger, Faye.
Note 2: Sharon has: Mary Wilma, b. 22 May 1894, d. 26 June 1896

41   iii.   **Trace L. SCHWYHART** was born in 1898 in Ohio.
Note 1: Wheeling Twp, Guernsey Co, OH: 1920, 22
Note 2: Sharon does not have this child listed.

42   iv.   **Alta M. SCHWYHART** was born in 1901 in Ohio.
Note 1: Wheeling Twp, Guernsey Co, OH: 1920, 19
Note 2: Sharon has: Alta M., b 10 Oct 1900, d. 27 March 1976

Third Generation

13. **Jennie LEWIS** (Mary Jane SCHWYHART-2, Jacob-1) was born in Nov 1878 in Ohio.
Note 1: 1900 U. S. census

Jennie Lewis married Jacob WEARSCH – details sought.

Jacob WEARSCH was born in 1878 in Ohio.
Note 1: 1920 U. S. census

Jennie LEWIS and Jacob WEARSCH had the following children:

> 43   i. **Lewis WEARSCH** was born in 1905 in Ohio.
>   Note 1: 1920 U. S. census

15. **Wilma Sue LEWIS** (Mary Jane SCHWYHART-2, Jacob-1) was born in Jan 1884 in Ohio.
Note 1: Sandi Share, Mar 2006
Note 2: 1900 U. S. census
Note 3: Philip Wearsch found in:
U.S. Atlantic and Great Lakes - Census Index (1880)
   State: Ohio
   County: Lorain
   Township: Avon
   Relationship to Head: Son
   Age: 6
   Gender: Male
   Race: White
   Marital Status: Single
   Birthplace: OHIO
   Birth Year: <1874>
   Mother Birthplace: BAVARIA
   Father Birthplace: PRUSSIA
   Roll: T9_1042
   Page: 337D
   ED: 162   [from Genealogy.com]

Wilma Sue LEWIS and Philip Christopher WEARSCH were married in 1903.
Note 1: 1910 U. S. census

Philip Christopher WEARSCH was born in 1874 in Ohio. He died in 1956. Philip Wearsch found in:
Note 1: U.S. Atlantic and Great Lakes - Census Index (1880)
   State: Ohio
   County: Lorain
   Township: Avon
   Relationship to Head: Son
   Age: 6
   Gender: Male
   Race: White
   Marital Status: Single
   Birthplace: OHIO
   Birth Year: <1874>

Mother Birthplace: BAVARIA
Father Birthplace: PRUSSIA
Roll: T9_1042
Page: 337D
ED: 162   [from Genealogy.com]

Wilma Sue LEWIS and Philip Christopher WEARSCH had the following children:

44	i.	**Mary Elizabeth WEARSCH** was born in 1904 in Ohio. She died in 1983. Note 1: 1910 U. S. census
+45	ii.	**Charles Gordon WEARSCH**, born in 1906, Ohio; married Barbara I. HUTTON, in 1927; died in Jul 1977. Note 1: 1930 U. S. census
46	iii.	**Lillis Ruth WEARSCH** was born in 1908 in Ohio. Note 1: 1910 U. S. census
47	iv.	**Robert Lewis WEARSCH** was born on 27 Apr 1910 in Ohio. He died on 17 Feb 1988. Note 1: Sandi Share, Mar 2006. Note 2: At Ancestry. Com, 26 Apr 2005
+48	v.	**Doris WEARSCH**, born in 1914.
49	vi.	**Walter Hayes WEARSCH** was born in 1917 in Ohio. Note 1: Sandi Share, Mar 2006 Note 2: 1930 U. S. census

18. **Charles H. SCHWYHART** (William A.-2, Jacob-1) was born in Nov 1882 in Ohio.
Note 1: Wheeling Twp, Guernsey Co, OH: 1900, 17, with birth date and state
Note 2: 1910 census, Coshocton, Coshocton Co, OH, has Charles Schwyhart, 29, OH, with wife (not named), 30, M1 5 1 1 , OH3, and daughter (not named), 3.

Charles H. SCHWYHART married Unknown UNKNOWN – details sought.

Unkonwn UNKNOWN was born in 1880 in Ohio.

Charles H. SCHWYHART and Unkonwn UNKNOWN had the following children:

| 50 | i. | **Unknown SCHWYHART** was born in 1907 in Ohio. |

20. **Luella (Lestie)(Lesta) SCHWYHART** (William A.-2, Jacob-1) was born in Feb 1892 in Kimbolton, Ohio. She died on 16 Nov 1989 in St. Petersburg, Pinella County, Florida.
Note 1: Wheeling Twp, Guernsey Co, OH: 1900, 8, with birth date and state
Listed as 'Lestie' in 1910 census with parent.

Luella (Lestie)(Lesta) SCHWYHART and J. Carl MCCLAUGHRY were married in Guernsey Cem, Guernsey Co, Ohio.

J. Carl MCCLAUGHRY (son of Elsworth MCCLAUGHRY and M. Blanche UNKNOWN) was born on 2 Nov 1889. He died in Jun 1973 in St. Petersburg, Pinella County, Florida.

Luella (Lestie)(Lesta) SCHWYHART and J. Carl MCCLAUGHRY had the following children:

+51   i.   **Robert Harold MCCLAUGHRY**, born on 29 Jan 1925; died on 2 Jan 2006.

+52   ii.   **Mary MCCLAUGHRY**, married R. C. CARMAN.

22. **Mossie A. (Mossagate) SCHWYHART** (John C.-2, Jacob-1) was born in Jun 1886 in Kansas.
Note 1: Federal census, Belle Plaine Twp, Sumner Co, Kansas for 1900, 1910, 1920, 13, 22, not listed.
Note 2: True name from Doug Carr Packet, July 2008

Mossie A. (Mossagate) SCHWYHART and Chester Arthur MASON were married.

Chester Arthur MASON - details sought.
Note 1: Doug Carr Schwyhart North packet, July 2008.

23. **Harrison Earl SCHWYHART** (John C.-2, Jacob-1) was born on 11 Jul 1890 in Oklahoma. He died in Jun 1963 in Kansas.
Note 1: Doug Carr Schwyhart North packet, July 2008.
Note 2: Federal census, Belle Plaine Twp, Sumner Co, Kansas for 1900, 1910, 1920, 9, 19, 29.
Note 3: 1930 census for KS, Cowley Co, Udall, has: Harison E. Schwyhart, 39, M at 35, OH, farm laborer, with wife, Vera V, 30, M at 25, KS, and son, Henry D., 2, KS.
Note 4: Harrison Davis, of Wellington, KS, listed as part of the Kansas 353rd Infantry Regiment, Company C, American Expeditionary Forces, World War I, rank not shown.
Note 5: SSDI has Harrison SCHUYHART (Gen.com), b. 11 Jul 1890, d. Jun 1963, KS, issued KS (no last res)
Note 5: Harrison Earl, same date, per Doug Carr Packet, July 2008

Harrison Earl SCHWYHART and Alice Fae WHITNEY were married.

Alice Fae WHITNEY – more details sought.
Note 1: First wife of Harrison, per Doug Carr Packet, July 2008

Harrison Earl SCHWYHART and Veva Venita BEAVER were married in 1925.

Veva Venita BEAVER (daughter of William Henry BEAVER and Nannie Alice HORNBEEK) was born on 6 Jun 1899 in KS. She died on 14 Nov 1984 in Wichita, KS.
Note 1: Details found on Genealogy.com, on a Family Home Page.
Note 2: SSDI has birth and death dates, also, under Veva.

Harrison Earl SCHWYHART and Veva Venita BEAVER had the following children:

+53   i.   **Henry D. SCHWYHART**, born on 18 May 1927, Udall, Cowley Co, KS; married Marilyn RICE, on 6 Jun 1948; died on 8 Mar 2004, Udall, Cowley Co, KS.

Note 1: On 26 Apr 2005:
http://www.ancestry.com/search/obit/view.aspx?kw=schwyhart+Henry+Darwin&pid=3118597&
url=http://search.ancestry.com/cgi-bin/sse.dll%3Fdb%3dweb-
obituary%252c%26gsfn%3dHenry%2bDarwin%26gsln%3dschwyhart%26sx%3d%26year%3d
%26yearend%3d%26gskw%3d%26gsco%3d1%26gspl%3d1%252c%2b%26prox%3d1%26rank
%3d0%26ti%3d0%26ti.si%3d0%26gss%3dangs%26submit.x%3d22%26submit.y%3d11, and
http://www.winfieldcourier.com/obit/o040319.html#6153.

24. Paul Dewey SCHWYHART (John C.-2, Jacob-1) was born on 24 Oct 1892 in Oklahoma
(Indian Territory).
Note 1: Doug Carr Schwyhart North packet, July 2008.
Note 2: Federal census, Belle Plaine Twp, Sumner Co, Kansas for 1900, 1910, 1920, 6, 17, 26.
Note 3: SSDI has Paul D Schwyhart, b. 24 Oct 1892, d. 3 May 1989, Mulvane, Sumner, KS.
Issued KS.
Note 4: SSDI also has Paul D Schwyhart, b. 1 Aug 1922, d. 24 Jan 2003, Mulvane, Sumner, KS,
Issued KS. Assume this is a son...

Bertha Estelle LOPER - more information sought.
Note 1: Doug Carr Schwyhart North packet, July 2008.

Paul Dewey SCHWYHART and Bertha Estelle LOPER had the following children:

54   i.   **Paul D. SCHWYHART** was born on 1 Aug 1922. He died on 24 Jan 2003
                 in Mulvane, Sumner Co, KS.
                 Note 1: SSDI has birth and death dates.

25. Ida Marie SCHWYHART (John C.-2, Jacob-1) was born on 21 Mar 1895 in Kansas.
Federal census, Belle Plaine Twp, Sumner Co, Kansas for 1900, 1910, 1920, 5, 15, not listed.
[listed as Idell M. (Ida)]
Note 1: Doug Carr Schwyhart North packet, July 2008.

Ida Marie SCHWYHART and Arthur Gilbert HUNT were married.

Arthur Gilbert HUNT - more information sought.
Note 1: Doug Carr Schwyhart North packet, July 2008.

29. Helen Elnora SCHWYHART (John C.-2, Jacob-1) was born on 23 Jun 1906 in Belle
Plaine, Sumner Co, Kansas.
Note 1: Doug Carr Schwyhart North packet, July 2008.
Note 2: Federal census, Belle Plaine Twp, Sumner Co, Kansas for 1910, 1920, 2, 13.
Note 3: Helen born at The Home Place, northeast of Belle Plaine, Sumner Co, KS

Helen Elnora SCHWYHART and Glen Elias CARR were married.

Glen Elias CARR – more information sought.
Note 1: Doug Carr Schwyhart North packet, July 2008.

Helen Elnora SCHWYHART and Glen Elias CARR had the following children:

+55   i. **David's Father CARR**, married David's Mother UNKNOWN.

31. **Gladys SCHWYHART** (Isaac N.-2, Jacob-1) was born on 31 May 1911 in Ohio. She died on 31 Jan 1982.
Note 1: Wheeling Twp, Guernsey Co, OH: 1920, 8
Note 2: Sharon has: Gladys Irene, b. 31 May 1911, d. 31 Jan 1931, Charles Braniger (Charles is the great uncle who wrote down the information that I have)

Gladys SCHWYHART and Charles BRANIGER were married in Sep 1931.

Charles BRANIGER – more information sought.

34. **Eva Belle SCHWYHART** (Joseph Thomas-2, Jacob-1) was born on 26 Oct 1880. She died on 9 Apr 1957. She was buried in Kimbolton Cemetery, OH.

John Franklin BARTHELOW (son of George BARTHELOW and Armantha STOTLER) was born on 31 Dec 1876. He died on 16 Oct 1946. He was buried in Kimbolton Cemetery, OH.

Eva Belle SCHWYHART and John Franklin BARTHELOW had the following children:

56   i. **Theresa BARTHELOW** was born on 9 Nov 1901. She died on 25 Jun 1974.
+57   ii. **Harry C. BARTHELOW**, born on 7 Dec 1906; married Bessie W. KENNEDY, on 22 Dec 1947; died on 11 Feb 1973.

35. **Maud A. SCHWYHART** (Joseph Thomas-2, Jacob-1) was born in Jun 1881 in Ohio. She died on 14 Jul 1969. She was buried in Northwood Cemetery, Cambridge, OH.
Note 1: Liberty Twp, Guernsey Co, OH: 1900, 18, with birth date and state.

Maud A. SCHWYHART married J. Lewis YAW – more information sought.

J. Lewis YAW died in Jul 1957. He was buried on 23 Jul 1957 in Northwood Cemetery, Cambridge, OH.

Maud A. SCHWYHART and J. Lewis YAW had the following children:

+58   i. **Edith YAW**, born on 4 Mar 1907; died on 7 Nov 1997.

36. **Naphtali (Naph) SCHWYHART** (Joseph Thomas-2, Jacob-1) was born in Apr 1885 in Ohio. He died on 22 Apr 1954. He was buried in Northwood Cemetery, Cambridge, OH.
Note 1: Liberty Twp, Guernsey Co, OH: 1900, 15, with birth date and state
Note 2: 1910 census, Ohio, Guernsey Co, Cambridge, 1st Ward, Prec B, has Naph, 24, M1 3 OH3, R. R. Rem Road, w/wife, Mae, 28, M2 3 1 1 OH3, and son, Eugene, 2.

Naphtali (Naph) SCHWYHART and Lillian 'Mae' WILSON were married in 1907.

Lillian 'Mae' WILSON was born in 1882 in Ohio. She died in Sep 1952. She was buried on 17 Sep 1952 in Northwood Cemetery, Cambridge, OH.

Naphtali (Naph) SCHWYHART and Lillian 'Mae' WILSON had the following children:

+59	i.	**Eugene W. SCHWYHART**, born on 10 Feb 1908, Ohio; married Margaret BOYD, on 20 Dec 1930; died on 18 Oct 1956.
+60	ii.	**Helen F. SCHWYHART**, born on 13 Apr 1924; died on 2 May 1980.

37. **Mary 'Bernice' SCHWYHART** (Joseph Thomas-2, Jacob-1) was born on 5 Feb 1889 in Ohio. She died in Apr 1968.
Liberty Twp, Guernsey Co, OH: 1900, 11, with birth date and state.

Mary 'Bernice' SCHWYHART married J. Leonard WARDEN – more details sought.

J. Leonard WARDEN was born in 1886. He was buried on 9 Sep 1948 in Northwood Cemetery, Cambridge, OH. He died in Sep 1948.

Mary 'Bernice' SCHWYHART and J. Leonard WARDEN had the following children:

61	i.	**Clyde WARDEN** was born on 15 Jun 1908. He died on 23 Mar 1986. He was buried in Northwood Cemetery, Cambridge, OH.
+62	ii.	**J. Craig WARDEN**, born on 5 Jun 1910; married Edna STRINGFELLOW, on 11 Aug 1938; died on 8 Aug 1974.
63	iii.	**Dr. Carl WARDEN** was born on 10 Aug 1913. He died in Dec 1982.
64	iv.	**Dr. Clair WARDEN** was born in 1921. He died on 7 Jan 1985. He was buried in Northwood Cemetery, Cambridge, OH.

38. **Joseph 'Ralph' SCHWYHART** (Joseph Thomas-2, Jacob-1) was born on 29 May 1894 in Liberty Twp, Guernsey Co, Ohio. He died on 18 Dec 1975 in Guernsey Co, Ohio. He was buried in Northwood Cemetery, Cambridge, OH.
Note 1: Liberty Twp, Guernsey Co, OH: 1900, 6, with birth date and state; 1910, 15, 1920, 25.
Note 2: Also, have email from Guernsey Co with death and marriage information.
Note 1: 1930 census for Massillon, Stark Co, OH, has: J. Ralph Schwyhart, 33, Lelia, 30, Kathryn I., 11, Elizabeth, 10, Edna M., 8, Bonnie J., 3.
Note 3: SSDI has birth and death dates, as well.

Joseph 'Ralph' SCHWYHART and Lelia Kathryn KENNEDY were married on 28 Jun 1916 in Cambridge, Guernsey Co, Ohio.

Lelia Kathryn KENNEDY (daughter of William B. KENNEDY and Clarissa Ann MCCULLOUGH) was born on 3 Dec 1898. She died in May 1979 in Akron, Summit Co, OH. She was buried in Northwood Cemetery, Cambridge, OH.
Note1: SSDI has Lelia Schwyhart, b. 3 Dec 1898, d. May 1979, Akron, Summit Co, OH.

Joseph 'Ralph' SCHWYHART and Lelia Kathryn KENNEDY had the following children:

65	i.	**Catherine 'Eileen' SCHWYHART** was born on 3 Aug 1918 in Ohio.

                      Note 1: 10/12 in 1920 census

65 i. Catherine 'Eileen' SCHWYHART was born on 3 Aug 1918 in Ohio.
Note 1: 10/12 in 1920 census
Note 2: Melba has her name as Kathy 'Eileen'
Note 3: Catherine I. in 1930 census.

66 ii. Elizabeth Ann SCHWYHART was born on 17 Mar 1920.

+67 iii. Edna Mae SCHWYHART, born on 12 Aug 1921; married Leonard D. ACKLEY, on 20 Oct 1943; died on 20 Jan 1994.

68 iv. Bonnie Jean SCHWYHART was born on 8 Oct 1926.

39. **Lillis Grace SCHWYHART** (Lemuel G.-2, Jacob-1) was born on 13 May 1897. She died on 4 Sep 1980.
Note 1: Guernsey Co Gen Soc, 10 Jun 1996 packet, Gibson Family Records, Martha Gibson #3504, married Lemuel and then I.N. Says children by Lemuel are Grace, Alta, Wilma; children my I.N. are Ruth, Child m. Charles Braniger, Faye.
Note 2: Lillis Grace per Sharon

Lillis Grace SCHWYHART and Clarence Peiter HILL were married on 12 Nov 1921.

Clarence Peiter HILL was born on 14 Sep 1894. He died on 2 Aug 1964.

Lillis Grace SCHWYHART and Clarence Peiter HILL had the following children:

69 i. James Roy HILL was born on 20 Apr 1923. He died on 26 Jul 1930.
Note 1: Sharon adds, after death date: (kicked in the head by a horse)

+70 ii. Martha Forest HILL, born on 14 Apr 1924; married Walter B. MILLER, on 3 Aug 1947; died on 27 Apr 1986.

71 iii. Fred Raymond HILL was born on 2 Aug 1925. He died in Jun 1985.
Note 1: Sharon says, after death date: Unmarried

Chapter 8

William Z. SCHWYHART and His Descendants

First Generation

1. **William Z. SCHWYHART** was born in 1821 in Belmont Co, Ohio. He died in 1862. He was buried in Steel Cemetery, Logan Co, Ohio.
Note 1: 1860 census, Bokes Creek Twp, Logan Co, Ohio: 59, OH
Note 2: Per Karen Nucci info 6 Sep 1999: b. 1821, not 1801! If so, fits here. Does match wife age better (1819).
Note 3: 1922 History of Daviess and Gentry Counties Missouri, pp. 745-46: Sketch of the "capable and well known police judge of Gallatin." - M.S. son of William Z. - said in sketch to have been born in 1816 in Belmont Co, OH, and died in 1862. His wife was born in 1817 and died on April 15, 1862. They are buried in Steel Cemetery, Logan Co, OH.
Note 4: 1850 census, Logan Co, OH: William, 29, Ruth 31, Marion, 4, Henry, 3, Landon, 1, James, b. 22 (all born in OH).

William Z. SCHWYHART and Ruth ROBERTS were married on 21 Dec 1843 in Guernsey Co, Ohio.

Ruth ROBERTS was born between 1817 and 1819 in Ohio. She died on 15 Apr 1862. She was buried in Steel Cemetery, Logan Co, Ohio.
Note 1: 1860 census, Bokes Creek Twp, Logan Co, Ohio: 41, OH
Note 2: Roberts surname Per Karen Nucci info 6 Sep 1999, and marriage info
Note 3: 1922 History of Daviess and Gentry Counties Missouri, pp. 745-46: Sketch of the "capable and well known police judge of Gallatin." - see comments on William Z. notes (her husband).

William Z. SCHWYHART and Ruth ROBERTS had the following children:

+2	i.	**Landon SCHWYHART**, born in May 1845, Ohio; married Nancy E. UNKNOWN, in 1866; died before 1922.	
+3	ii.	**Marion S. (M._S.) SCHWYHART**, born on 10 May 1845, Guernsey Co, Ohio; married Unknown SWOFFORD, on 21 Mar 1912, Gallatin, Daviess Co, Missouri.	
+4	iii.	**Henry SCHWYHART**, born in 1847, Ohio; died before 1922.	
5	iv.	**Armanda (Arminda) SCHWYHART** was born in 1852 in Ohio. She died after 1922.	

Note 1: 1860 census, Bokes Creek Twp, Logan Co, Ohio: 59, OH
Note 2: 1922 History of Daviess and Gentry Counties Missouri, pp. 745-46: Sketch of the "capable and well known police judge of Gallatin." - her brother - it says: Arminda, living in Los Angeles, Calif.
Note 3: 1930 census, Rushsylvania, Rushcreek Twp, Logan Co, OH, has

Arminda Schwyhart, 79, Wd, OH.

Second Generation

2. **Landon SCHWYHART** (William Z.-1) was born in May 1845 in Ohio. He died before 1922.
Note 1: 1860 census, Bokes Creek Twp, Logan Co, Ohio: 11, OH Gallatin, Marion Twp, Daviess Co, MO, census: 1900, 50, MO
Note 2: 1870 census, Marion twp, Daviess Co, MO, Landon, 21, Nancy, 20, and his sister, Arminda, 19, OH.
Note 3: 1922 History of Daviess and Gentry Counties Missouri, pp. 745-46: Sketch of the "capable and well known police judge of Gallatin." - brother.
Note 4: 1910 Census, MO, Davies Co, Union twp, Landon, 65, M1 44 Own Income, with Nancy E, 58, M1 44, 2 0, IN3, with 2 Boarders.
Note 5: 1880 census for Marion, Daviess Co, MO, has: Landon, 30, OH, with wife, Nancy, 28, IN.

Landon SCHWYHART and Nancy E. UNKNOWN were married in 1866.

Nancy E. UNKNOWN was born in Oct 1851 in Indiana.
Note 1: Gallatin, Marion Twp, Daviess Co, MO, census: 1900, 48, IN
Note 2: Had two children, neither living in 1910.

3. **Marion S. (M._S.) SCHWYHART** (William Z.-1) was born on 10 May 1845 in Guernsey Co, Ohio.
Note 1: 1860 census, Bokes Creek Twp, Logan Co, Ohio: 15, OH; 1880, 34 1900 census, Marion Twp, Daviess Co, MO: 55, birth month and year, state. 1910, 64; 1920, 74
Note 2: 1922 History of Daviess and Gentry Counties Missouri, pp. 745-46: Sketch of the "capable and well known police judge of Gallatin." - M. S. Schwyhart was reared in Logan County, OH, near Ridgeway. He received his education in the district schools. During the Civil War, Mr. Schwyhart enlisted on June 3, 1862, in the army and served for three months, after which he re-enlisted and served throughout the war. He served in Company H, 96th Ohio Volunteer Infantry, and was wounded on April 8, 1964, at Sabine Cross Roads in Louisiana on the Red River. He was taken prisoner and after three months paroled and returned to the Federal lines at Mouth River after the war. After the war, Mr. Schwyhart removed to Daviess County, MO, settling in Marion Township, where he remained on a farm until 1911. He then retired and moved to Gallatin; he was elected judge of the police court in 1919, which office he now holds.
Note 3: Continues about 2nd wife, after first wife and children info.

Jane BUSH was born in Jul 1847 in Indiana.
Note 1: 1900 census, Marion Twp, Daviess Co, MO: 52, birth month and year, state. 1880, 32, IN
Note 2: 1922 History of Daviess and Gentry Counties Missouri, pp. 745-46: Sketch of the "capable and well known police judge of Gallatin." - "...(he) married the first time to Miss Bush,

a daughter of William and Jane C. Bush, natives of Berkshire County, Mass."

Marion S. (M._S.) SCHWYHART and Jane BUSH had the following children:

+6   i. **Albert H. SCHWYHART**, born on 7 Oct 1868, Daviess Co, Missouri; married Ella UNKNOWN, in 1898; died on 17 Jun 1913.

+7   ii. **William W. SCHWYHART**, born on 24 Sep 1870, Daviess Co, Missouri.

+8   iii. **Walter A. SCHWYHART**, born on 20 Jul 1872, Daviess Co, Missouri; died on 8 Jul 1944, Lane Co, OR.

+9   iv. **Claudius M. (Claude) SCHWYHART**, born on 23 Sep 1874, Daviess Co, Missouri; died in Apr 1965.

+10   v. **Herbert C. SCHWYHART**, born on 15 Feb 1876, Daviess Co, Missouri; married Laura M. BALDWIN, in 1901.

11   vi. **Roy M. SCHWYHART** was born on 3 Jun 1879 in Daviess Co, Missouri. Marion Twp, Daviess Co, MO, census: 1880, 1, 1900 (on own)
Note 1: 1922 History of Daviess and Gentry Counties Missouri, pp. 745-46: Sketch of the "capable and well known police judge of Gallatin."

+12   vii. **Everett SCHWYHART**, born on 5 Feb 1887, Daviess Co, Missouri; died on 11 Sep 1941, Kansas City, Jackson Co, MO.

Marion S. (M._S.) SCHWYHART and Unknown SWOFFORD were married on 21 Mar 1912 in Gallatin, Daviess Co, Missouri.

Unknown SWOFFORD (daughter of John S. SWOFFORD and Ann BINION) was born on 9 Nov 1865 in Daviess Co, Missouri. She died after 1922.
Note 1: 1922 History of Daviess and Gentry Counties Missouri, pp. 745-46: Sketch of the "capable and well known police judge of Gallatin." (he) married second Miss Swofford.

4. **Henry SCHWYHART** (William Z.-1) was born in 1847 in Ohio. He died before 1922.
1860 census, Bokes Creek Twp, Logan Co, Ohio: 13, OH
Note 1: 1922 History of Daviess and Gentry Counties Missouri, pp. 745-46: Sketch of the "capable and well known police judge of Gallatin." - brother.
Note 2: 1870 census, MO, Daviess Co, Marion Twp, listed as Herry Schuyhart (gen.com), 24, OH, with wife, Harriett E. 25, MO, and children, William R., 3 (M), and Ruth M., 1, MO. Several Fields families living nearby!!

Harriett FIELDS – more information sought.
Note 1: Per Karen Nucci information, 6 Sep 1999

Henry SCHWYHART and Harriett FIELDS had the following children:

13   i. **Willam R. SCHWYHART** was born in 1867 in Missouri.

14   ii. **Ruth M. SCHWYHART** was born in 1869 in Missouri.

Third Generation

6. **Albert H. SCHWYHART** (Marion S. (M._S.)-2, William Z.-1) was born on 7 Oct 1868 in Daviess Co, Missouri. He died on 17 Jun 1913.
Note 1: Marion Twp, Daviess Co, MO, census: 1880, 10, 1900, 31 (on own)
Note 2: 1922 History of Daviess and Gentry Counties Missouri, pp. 745-46: Sketch of the "capable and well known police judge of Gallatin."
Note 3: See: http://caselaw.lp.findlaw.com/scripts/getcase.pl?court=us&vol=227&invol=184 for lawsuit settled in Feb 1913, for injuries by railroad (Google Search, 26, Apr 2005)

Albert H. SCHWYHART and Ella UNKNOWN were married in 1898.

Ella UNKNOWN was born in Nov 1866 in Missouri.
Note 1: Jefferson Twp, Daviess Co, MO, census: 1900, 33, MO
Note 2: 1900 census, Missouri, Daviess Co, Jefferson Twp: Albert H., Oct 1868, 31, M2, MO, OH, WI, RR Laborer (Section), with wife Ella, Nov 1866, 33, M2 0 0 MO2 KY.
Note 3: 1910 census, Missouri, Daviess Co, Jefferson Twp: Albert H., 41, M1 12, MO OH, WI, Clerk Food Store, with wife, Ella, 44, M1 12, 0 0 MO2 KY.

7. **William W. SCHWYHART** (Marion S. (M._S.)-2, William Z.-1) was born on 24 Sep 1870 in Daviess Co, Missouri.
Note 1: Marion Twp, Daviess Co, MO, census: 1880, 9, 1900, 29
Note 2: 1922 History of Daviess and Gentry Counties Missouri, pp. 745-46: Sketch of the "capable and well known police judge of Gallatin."
Note 3: 1910 census, for Colorado, LaPlata Co, Farmer, New Farm, 43, M1 9, MO, OH, MO, with Wife, Helen, 30, M1 9 3 3 , Eng3 (naturalized in 1884), and 3 daughter (all CO): Isabelle, 7, Mary 5, Edith 2.

William W. SCHWYHART married Helen UNKNOWN – more details sought.

Helen UNKNOWN was born in 1880.
Note 1: 1930 Census for Lafayette, Boulder Co, CO, has: Helen Schwyhart, HD, 50, PA, with daughter Edith, 22, and Luciel, 19.

William W. SCHWYHART and Helen UNKNOWN had the following children:

15	i.	**Isabelle SCHWYHART** was born in 1903 in Colorado.
16	ii.	**Mary SCHWYHART** was born in 1905 in Colorado.
17	iii.	**Edith SCHWYHART** was born in 1908 in Colorado.
18	iv.	**Lucile SCHWYHART** was born in 1911 in Colorado.

8. **Walter A. SCHWYHART** (Marion S. (M._S.)-2, William Z.-1) was born on 20 Jul 1872 in Daviess Co, Missouri. He died on 8 Jul 1944 in Lane Co, OR.
Note 1: Marion Twp, Daviess Co, MO, census: 1880, 8, 1900, 29 (on own)
Note 2: 1922 History of Daviess and Gentry Counties Missouri, pp. 745-46: Sketch of the "capable and well known police judge of Gallatin."

Note 3: 1920 Soundex Kansas: Walter A. Schwyhart, 47, Cheyenne Co (NW corner), wife, Lydia, 49, IL, Virgil, S, 20, MO, Mildred, D, 16, MO.
Note 4: 1930 census for Englewood, Arapahoe Co, CO, has: Walter A. Schwyhart, 57, MO, with wife, Lyuba A., 58, and son, Virgil D., 30.
Note 5: Oregon Death Index, 1903-98, Lane Co, 8 Jul 1944. (Eugene is in Lane Co)

Lydia A. SHIPLEY was born on 4 Feb 1872 in Cook Co, Illinois. She died on 15 Nov 1962 in Eugene, Oregon.
Note 1: Marion Twp, Daviess Co, MO, census: 1900, 28, MO
Note 2: Death listed in Oregon Death Index, 1903-98, Lane Co, 5 N 1962, Certificate 14604 (Eugene is in Lane Co)

Walter A. SCHWYHART and Lydia A. SHIPLEY had the following children:

+19	i.	**Virgil D. SCHWYHART**, born in Nov 1899, Missouri; married Jane Ann HEBERLING, on 23 Aug 1932, Glenwood Springs, CO; died on 10 Dec 1957, Grand Junction, Mesa Co, CO.
20	ii.	**Mildred SCHWYHART** was born in 1904 in Missouri. Cheyenne Co, MO Note 1: Census: 1920, 16, MO

9. **Claudius M. (Claude) SCHWYHART** (Marion S. (M._S.)-2, William Z.-1) was born on 23 Sep 1874 in Daviess Co, Missouri. He died in Apr 1965.
Note 1: Marion Twp, Daviess Co, MO, census: 1900, 25; 1920, 45, with daughter
Note 2: 1922 History of Daviess and Gentry Counties Missouri, pp. 745-46: Sketch of the "capable and well known police judge of Gallatin."
Note 3: 1910 census with father, 35 Widowed, with daughter, Mabel L. 11.
Note 4: SSDI has Claude, b. 23 Sep 1874, d. Apr 1965, (no last res), issues MO.

Claudius M. (Claude) SCHWYHART married Unknown UNKNOWN – more information sought.

Unknown UNKNOWN – more information sought.

Claudius M. (Claude) SCHWYHART and Unknown UNKNOWN had the following children:

21	i.	**Mabel L. SCHWYHART** was born in Feb 1899 in Missouri. Note 1: Marion Twp, Daviess Co, MO, census: 1900, 1, MO; 1910, 11, 1920, 20 Note 2: Listed as Mabel L., 11, on 1910 census. Note 3: In 1900, listed as Mabelle, Feb 1899.

10. **Herbert C. SCHWYHART** (Marion S. (M._S.)-2, William Z.-1) was born on 15 Feb 1876 in Daviess Co, Missouri.
Note 1: Marion Twp, Daviess Co, MO, census: 1880, 3, 1900 (on own)
Note 2: 1922 History of Daviess and Gentry Counties Missouri, pp. 745-46: Sketch of the "capable and well known police judge of Gallatin."

Note 3: 1900, IA, Tama Co, Lincoln Twp, Employee, Farm Laborer, B. Feb 1876, 24, S.
Note 4: 1910 census, same location, Herbert 36, M9, MO, OH, IN, Farmer, with wife, Laura, 28, M9 3 3 , IA, IL, NY, with Clyde L., 7, Earnest W., 5, and Robert, 2.
Note 5: 1920 Iowa, Grundy Co, Washington Twp, Herbert C., 43, Farmer, and Laura M., 38, and Clyde L, 17, Walter E., 14, Robert M, 121, and May E., 9.
Note 6: 1930 Iowa, Grundy Co, Washington Twp, has: Herbert C., 54, M at 25, MO OH IN, Farmer, with Laura M., 48, M at 20, IA, IL, NY, and children, E. Walter, 25, (all IA, MO, IA), Robert M., 22, and Mary E., 19.

Herbert C. SCHWYHART and Laura M. BALDWIN were married in 1901.

Laura M. BALDWIN was born on 16 May 1881 in Iowa. She died in Sep 1970 in Grundy Center, Grundy Co, IA.
Note 1: SSDI has Laura Schwyhart, b. 16 May 1881, d. Sep 1970, Grundy Center, Grundy Co, IA (Issued IA 1956 and 1957).
Note 2: Maiden name is Baldwin, per daughter Mary's obit.

Herbert C. SCHWYHART and Laura M. BALDWIN had the following children:

22	i.	**Clyde L. SCHWYHART** was born in 1903 in Iowa.
		Note 1: With parents in 1920, 17, and 1910, 7, IA, MO, IA.
23	ii.	**E. Walter SCHWYHART** was born on 30 Mar 1905. He died on 19 Apr 1989 in Shell Rock, Butler Co, IA.
		Note 1: E. Walter Schwyhart, 25, with parents in Washington Twp, Gundy Co, IA, in 1930 census.
		Note 2: Earnest W., 5, in 1910, IA, tama Co, Lincoln twp, with parents.
		Note 3: 1920 has Walter E., 14, IA, MO, IA, with parents.
		Note 4: SSDI has E W Schwyhart, b. 30 Mar 1905, d. 19 Apr 1989, Shell Rock, Butler Co, IA, issued IA.
24	iii.	**Robert M. SCHWYHART** was born on 3 Jan 1908 in Iowa. He died on 25 Sep 2001 in Tempe, Maricopa Co, AZ.
		Note 1: SSDI has a Robert M Schwyhart, b. 3 Jan 1908, d. 25 Sep 2001, Tempe, Maricopa, AZ (Issued IA, 1956 ad 1958).
+25	iv.	**Mary E. SCHWYHART**, born on 11 Oct 1910, Grundy Center, Grundy Co, IA; married Bliss WILLOUGHBY, on 15 Jul 1939; died on 22 Oct 2002, Burnsville, NC.
		Note 1: From Ancestry.com: Obituary Collection, 26 Oct 2005.

12. **Everett SCHWYHART** (Marion S. (M._S.)-2, William Z.-1) was born on 5 Feb 1887 in Daviess Co, Missouri. He died on 11 Sep 1941 in Kansas City, Jackson Co, MO. He was buried in Mount Washington Cemetery, Independence, Jackson Co, MO.
Note 1: Marion Twp, Daviess Co, MO, census: 1900, 13
Note 2: 1922 History of Daviess and Gentry Counties Missouri, pp. 745-46: Sketch of the "capable and well known police judge of Gallatin."

Maud M. KEITHLEY (daughter of John Franklin KEITHLEY and Mary Ellen SEATON) was born on 14 Feb 1887 in Taney Co, Missouri. She died on 6 Jun 1933 in Kansas City, MO. She

was buried in Mount Washington Cemetery, Independence, MO.
Note 1: 1408 Bellefonte Av, Kansas City, Jackson Co, MO, census: 1920, 32, MO: Last name and parents.

Everett SCHWYHART and Maud M. KEITHLEY had the following children:

+26   i. **Mary Francis SCHWYHART**, born on 27 Aug 1913, Missouri; married Charles E. WALSH; died on 3 May 1990.
      Note 1: Mary Francis Schwyhart Jul 2008 email.

James M. Schwyhart and family, in front of cabin;
near the White River where is now located Kimberling City and
Table Rock Lake, in Stone County, Missouri

Chapter 9

James M. SCHWYHART and His Descendants

First Generation

1. **James M. SCHWYHART** was born on 2 Feb 1827 in Belmont Co, Ohio. He died on 15 Jul 1900 in Stone Co, Missouri. He was buried in Philbert Cemetery, Kimberling City, Stone Co, Missouri.
Note 1: Gentry Co, Bogle Twp, MO, 1880 census, 53, OH - wife Susan Matilda James Twp,
Note 2: Stone Co, MO, 1900 census, 73, OH - Father born in PA, mother VA; wife, Elizabeth, MO, MO, MO, age 33, May 1867; James, Feb 1827
Note 3: Per Karen Nucci, Aug 1999: Death date, place of initial burial was Thomas Cemetery on the White River.
Note 4: Per Karen Nucci info 6 Sep 1999: son of Jacob and Sarah.
Note 5: Per B. Pitts Sheets, Sep 99; first marriage date and place.

James M. SCHWYHART first married Susan Matilda BELL on 8 May 1852 in Bellefontaine, Logan Co, Ohio.

Susan Matilda BELL was born in 1823 in Ohio.
Note 1: 1880 census, Bogle Twp, Gentry Co, MO, 57, OH
Note 2: 1870 census, Bogle Twp, Gentry Co, MO, 45, OH, with husband and 5 children; Albany P.O.

James M. SCHWYHART and Susan Matilda BELL had the following children:

+2	i.	**George Mitchell SCHWYHART**, born on 18 Jul 1853, Belmont Co, Ohio; married Margaret Elizabeth YOCUM, on 4 Nov 1891, Stone Co, Missouri; died on 3 Sep 1937, Baxter, Stone Co, Missouri.
3	ii.	**Mary E. SCHWYHART** was born about 1855. Note 1: Per B. Pitts Sheets, Sep 99.
+4	iii.	**Cyrus Bell SCHWYHART**, born on 2 May 1857, Ohio; married Alma May OLIVER, on 1 Jan 1893; died on 17 May 1932.
5	iv.	**John A. SCHWYHART** was born on 1 Mar 1859 in Ohio. Note 1: 1880 census, Bogle Twp, Gentry Co, MO, 21, OH Note 2: John Simon, per Karen Nucci, Aug 1999. Note 3: Per Karen Nucci info 6 Sep 1999: middle name (I had A.) Note 4: Per B. Pitts Sheets, Sep 99: He had A. also. Has birth date and state. Note 5: Affidavit at age 41 related to father's pension is signed John A. Schwyhart.
+6	v.	**Ceanith Anita SCHWYHART**, born on 26 Mar 1861, Logan Co, Ohio; married George A. RICHISON, on 31 Dec 1843, St. Louis, Missouri.

James M. SCHWYHART second married Elizabeth OVERSTREET on 11 Nov 1888 in Carroll Co, Arkansas.

Elizabeth OVERSTREET (daughter of George W. OVERSTREET and Mary A. RUCKMAN) was born on 5 May 1867 in Missouri. She died on 15 Aug 1902.
Note 1: James Twp, Stone Co, MO, 1900 census, May 1867, 33, MO MO MO
Note 2: Last Name per Karen Nucci, Aug 1999; also birth day, death info, her parents.
Note 3: George Washington Overstreet family from <vonda@peoplepc.com> Aug 2000 confirms details.

James M. SCHWYHART and Elizabeth OVERSTREET had the following children:

+7   i.   **Jeanette (Nettie) (Jennie) SCHWYHART**, born in Apr 1888, Missouri; married Thomas GORE, on 11 Feb 1904, Stone Co, Missouri.

8   ii.   **Emily S. (Ethel) SCHWYHART** was born on 24 Jan 1891 in Missouri. She died on 18 Feb 1963. She was buried in Philbert Cemetery, Kimberling City, Stone Co, Missouri.
Note 1: James Twp, Stone Co, MO, 1900 census, 10, MO, Jan 1890
Note 2: Gravestone in Philbert Cemetery, Kimberling City, MO says 24 Jan, 1891 - 18 Feb 1963, along with husband, Tony A, 10 Feb 1886 - 20 Apr 1972. _ Au 1999, have put Tony with Sarah, not Emily - dates are still in controversy.
Note 3: Per Karen Nucci infor, 6 Sep 1999: also known as Ethel in the family - adopted by James - believed to be a child of Elizabeth before she married James.

+9   iii.   **William Robert SCHWYHART**, born on 11 Nov 1892, Missouri; married Annie ALLEY, in 1918; died on 24 Nov 1964, McCarty Cemetery, Taney Co, Missouri.

+10   iv.   **Sarah A. (Sallie) SCHWYHART**, born on 25 Jan 1895, Missouri; married Antonio Augustus (Tony) HAMMERS, on 4 Jan 1913, Stone Co, MO; died on 18 Feb 1963.

+11   v.   **Elmer Ell SCHWYHART**, born on 3 Mar 1897, Marmaros, Stone Co, Missouri; married Martha Jane PITTS, on 17 Jan 1914, Stone Co, Missouri; died on 31 Jul 1975, Oroville, Butte Co, California.

12   vi.   **David Winchester SCHWYHART** was born on 11 Jul 1899 in Missouri. James Twp, Stone Co, MO, 1900 census, 11/12, MO, 11 in 1910.
Note 1: Name per Karen Nucci, Aug 1999: David Winchester, not just Winchester.

Second Generation

2. **George Mitchell SCHWYHART** (James M.-1) was born on 18 Jul 1853 in Belmont Co, Ohio. He died on 3 Sep 1937 in Baxter, Stone Co, Missouri.
Note 1: Death information from Karen Nucci, Aug 1999
Note 2: 1900 census, Missouri, Stone Co, James Twp, has: George, Jul 1853, 46, M8, OH3, Farmer; with wife, Margaret, Jul 1869, 30, M8, 5 5 , MO3; and children: John R., May 1890, 10,

(all MO,OH,MO), Mary A, Apr 1893, 7, James G., Feb 1895, 5, Joseph, Mar 1897, 3, William A., Oct 1899, 8/12, Susan M., mother, Jan 1821, wd, 6 5, OH, Ire, Va.

Note 3: 1910 census OK, Tulsa Co, Fry Twp: George, 55, M1 18, OH3, Farmer, with wife, Margaret, 46, M1 18, 7 7 , MO 3, and children: James G., 16 (all MO, OH. MO), Joe, 15, Willie A., 10, Anetia A., 7, Helen A., 4, and Wm M. Little, son-in-law, 25, M1 11/12, MO, TN, MO, and his wife, Matilda M., 17, M1 11/12, and their dau, Alma B. Little, 6/12, MO3.

Note 4: 1930 census for MO, Stone Co, White River twp, has George M, 76, OH, and Margaret E, 59, with son, Joe L., 33.

George Mitchell SCHWYHART and Margaret Elizabeth YOCUM were married on 4 Nov 1891 in Stone Co, Missouri.

Margaret Elizabeth YOCUM (daughter of Joseph YOCUM and Matilda GIBSON) was born on 15 Jun 1869 in Stone Co, Missouri. She died on 25 Feb 1947 in Baxter, Stone Co, Missouri.

Note 1: James Twp, Stone Co, MO, 1900 census, 30, MO; married 8 years, 5-5 listed, marriage date from Stone Co records.

Note 2: Karen Nucci, Aug 1999, has birth date as 15 Jun 1869, rather than Jul 1869 per census, in Stone Co, MO; d. 25 Feb 1947, Baxter, Stone Co, MO

George Mitchell SCHWYHART and Margaret Elizabeth YOCUM had the following children:

+13   i.   **(Riley) John Riley Yocum SCHWYHART**, born on 8 May 1890, Baxter, Stone Co, Missouri; married Lola TALIAFERRO, on 29 Aug 1920, Oklahoma; died on 14 Mar 1976, Tulsa, Tulsa Co, Oklahoma.

+14   ii.   **Matilda Alma Mary SCHWYHART**, born on 8 Apr 1893, Baxter, Stone Co, Missouri; married William Sherman LITTLE, on 29 Apr 1909; died on 9 Jan 1916.

+15   iii.   **James Garfield SCHWYHART**, born on 8 Feb 1895, Baxter, Stone Co, Missouri; died on 5 Apr 1978, Branson, Missouri.

+16   iv.   **Joseph Lincoln SCHWYHART**, born on 8 Mar 1897, Baxter, Stone Co, Missouri; married Irene HARGROVE, on 4 Mar 1941, Berryville, Carroll Co, Arkansas; died on 24 Mar 1985, Springfield, Missouri.

+17   v.   **William Aster SCHWYHART**, born on 2 Oct 1899, Baxter, Stone Co, Missouri; married Josie Bell YOKUM, on 9 Jul 1927, Berryville, Carroll Co, Arkansas; died in Jul 1973, Skaggs Hosp, Branson, Taney Co, Missouri.

+18   vi.   **Ceanith Anita SCHWYHART**, born on 22 Feb 1903, Baxter, Stone Co, Missouri.

+19   vii.   **Helen Agnes SCHWYHART**, born on 26 Sep 1906, Baxter, Stone Co, Missouri; married (Tony) Charles Edward Antonie PITTS, on 5 Oct 1940, Forsyth, Taney Co, Missouri; married Leuvoka Lee HARGROVE, on 26 Mar 1925, Baxter, Stone Co, Missouri; died on 26 Jul 1976, Pocatello, Bannock Co, Idaho.

4. Cyrus Bell SCHWYHART (James M.-1) was born on 2 May 1857 in Ohio. He died on 17 May 1932.

Note 1: Per Karen Nucci info 6 Sep 1999: Cyrus Bell - went to CO, is all the family knows, she says. Name only.

Note 2: Per B. Pitts Sheets, Sep 99: marriage and death dates, husband name.
Note 3: 1900 census, NE, Hitchcock Co, Trenton Village, has: Cyrus B. Schwyhart, May 1857, 43, M7, OH, PA, VA, Butcher, with wife, Alla M. , Apr 1874, 26, M7 3 2 , IN3, and Earl W., Jun 1895, 5, NE, OH, IN, and Myrtl W., Aug 1897, 2, NE, OH, IN.
Note 4: 1930 census for Arriola, Montezuma Co, CO, has: Cins B. Schwyhart, 73, Widowed, OH, PA, OH, Boarder.

Cyrus Bell SCHWYHART and Alma May OLIVER were married on 1 Jan 1893.

Alma May OLIVER was born in Apr 1874 in Indiana.
Note 1: James Sullivan, May 2008 emails.
Note 2: Per B. Pitts Sheets, Sep 99.
Note 3: Alla M., on 1900 census.
Note 4: Alma May per Jim Sullivan, May 2008 email

Cyrus Bell SCHWYHART and Alma May OLIVER had the following children:

20	i.	**Earl Wells SCHWYHART** was born on 7 Jan 1895 in Nebraska.
		Note 1: James Sullivan, May 2008 emails.
		Note 2: SSDI has Earl Schwyhart, b. 7 Jan 1895, d. Aug 1974, Tacoma, Pierce Co, WA, issued IN. Is this him?? - Per Jim, it appears this is the one!
		Note 3: Jim Sullivan has Earl Wells, b. 01,07,1895 and d. 1974
21	ii.	**Myrtl W. SCHWYHART** was born in Aug 1897 in Nebraska.

6. **Ceanith Anita SCHWYHART** (James M.-1) was born on 26 Mar 1861 in Logan Co, Ohio.
Note 1: 1880 census, Bogle Twp, Gentry Co, MO, 19, OH
Note 2: Per Karen Nucci information, 6 Sept 1999: Marriage and child info

Ceanith Anita SCHWYHART married James A. MARRS – more information sought.

James A. MARRS – more information sought.
Note 1: Per Karen Nucci sheets, Sep 1999: name.

Ceanith Anita SCHWYHART and James A. MARRS had the following children:

22	i.	**Agnes Alma MARRS** was born.
		Note 1: Per Karen Nucci sheets, Sep 1999: name and husband name
23	ii.	**Martha Ann Lenora MARRS** was born.
		Note 1: Per Karen Nucci sheets, Sep 1999: name and husband name

Ceanith Anita SCHWYHART and George A. RICHISON were married on 31 Dec 1843 in St. Louis, Missouri.

George A. RICHISON was born on 20 Oct 1860. He died on 5 Jan 1940.
Note 1: Per Karen Nucci sheets, Sep 1999: name and birth and death dates
Note 2: Per B. Pitts Sheets, Sep 99: Middle initial A.

7. Jeanette (Nettie) (Jennie) SCHWYHART (James M.-1) was born in Apr 1888 in Missouri. James Twp, Stone Co, MO, 1900 census, 12, MO 1920 census, 31
Note 1: Per Karen Nucci information, 6 Sep 1999: adopted by James, said to be earlier child of Elizabeth

Jeanette (Nettie) (Jennie) SCHWYHART and Thomas GORE were married on 11 Feb 1904 in Stone Co, Missouri.

Thomas GORE was born in 1885 in Missouri.
Note 1: James Twp, Stone Co, MO, 1920 census, MO VA MO
Note 2: Marriage in Stone Co, Book E, p. 314: 11 Feb 1904.

Jeanette (Nettie) (Jennie) SCHWYHART and Thomas GORE had the following children:

+24	i.	**Ethel GORE**, born in 1906, Missouri.
25	ii.	**Nellie GORE** was born in 1908 in Missouri.
		Note 1: James Twp, Stone Co, MO, 1920 census, 12, MO
26	iii.	**Hershal GORE** was born in 1910 in Missouri.
		Note 1: James Twp, Stone Co, MO, 1920 census, 10 , MO
27	iv.	**Winnie GORE** was born in 1913 in Missouri.
		Note 1: James Twp, Stone Co, MO, 1920 census, 7, MO
+28	v.	**Stella GORE**, born in 1916, Missouri.
29	vi.	**Blaine GORE** was born in 1917 in Missouri.
		Note 1: James Twp, Stone Co, MO, 1920 census, 2 8/12, MO
30	vii.	**Lavina GORE** was born in 1918 in Missouri.
		Note 1: James Twp, Stone Co, MO, 1920 census, 1 8/12, MO
		Note 2: Lavonia per Beulah.
31	viii.	**Eugene GORE** was born on 19 Feb 1928. He died on 27 Jul 1998.
		Note 1: SSDI has Eugene Gore, b. 19 Feb 1928, d. 27 Jul 1998, 95315 (Delhi, Merced Co, CA), issued OK.
32	ix.	**Jesse James GORE** – additional information sought.

9. William Robert SCHWYHART (James M.-1) was born on 11 Nov 1892 in Missouri. He died on 24 Nov 1964 in McCarty Cemetery, Taney Co, Missouri. He was buried in McCarty Cemetery, Taney Co, Missouri.
Note 1: James Twp, Stone Co, MO, 1900 census, 7, MO, Robert is listed.
Note 2: This is William R. !! Full Name per Karen Nucci, Aug 1999, and actual birth date. He served in WWI per Juli
Note 3: Buried at McCarth Cemetery, Taney County, Township 21, Range 19, Section 3, with wife Annie Schwyhart. Noted as: Mo Pvt 3 Co 164 Depot Brigade World War I
Note 4: William R. Schwyhart family appears in the 1930 census, in Cedar Creek Twp, Taney Co, MO: He 39, M 25, She, Anna, 28, M 18, Farmer, Gen Farm, with four children and mother-in-law, Rhoda Alley, 63, Wd. Children: Percy R., 10, Isaac W., 8, James O., 4, Lizzie R., 4/12.

William Robert SCHWYHART and Annie ALLEY were married in 1918.

Annie ALLEY was born on 29 Jun 1900. She died on 11 Sep 1994 in Hollister, Taney Co,

Missouri. She was buried in McCarty Cemetery, Taney Co, Missouri.
Note 1: Per Karen Nucci sheets, Sep 1999: Bob - birth and marriage to Annie, her birth and death date - 5 children
Note 2: Buried at McCarthy Cemetery, Taney County, Township 21, Range 19, Section 3, with husband William R. Schwyhart.
Note 3: SSDI has these dates, last res: Hollister, Taney Co, MO.

William Robert SCHWYHART and Annie ALLEY had the following children:

33	i.	**Percy R. SCHWYHART** was born in 1919. He died in 1931.
		Note 1: Believed to have died of appendicitis when he was about 12.
+34	ii.	**Isaac William (Ike) SCHWYHART**, born on 17 Dec 1921; married Betty MADISON, on 1 Jan 1948; died on 7 Aug 2003, Cedarville, Modoc Co, CA.
+35	iii.	**James Old (Jim) SCHWYHART**, born on 13 Jun 1925; died on 25 Oct 1977.
+36	iv.	**Lizzie R. SCHWYHART**, born on 16 Jul 1929.
+37	v.	**John SCHWYHART**, born on 18 Dec 1931; died on 2 Dec 1985.
+38	vi.	**Gene Ray SCHWYHART**, born on 5 Oct 1934.
+39	vii.	**Nora SCHWYHART**, born on 26 Mar 1937.
+40	viii.	**Mary SCHWYHART**, born on 25 Dec 1939.
+41	ix.	**Bobby J. SCHWYHART**, born in 1944/45; died on 14 Apr 2004, St. Louis, Missouri.

10. **Sarah A. (Sallie) SCHWYHART** (James M.-1) was born on 25 Jan 1895 in Missouri. She died on 18 Feb 1963. She was buried in Philbert Cemetery, Kimberling City, Stone Co, Missouri.
Note 1: James Twp, Stone Co, MO, 1900 census, 5, 14 in 1910, MO
Note 2: Birthday per Karen Nucci, Aug 1999; says she is Sally, married Tony Hammers, d. 1963, Stone Co, MO - controversy, stone says diff, diff from one census to another......
Note 3: Per Karen Nucci sheets, 8 Sept 1999: She says "Sally" - and her family.
Note 4: Berta says that Sallie was a school teacher (per Jean Hammers Janes and her daughter Carol Cron).
Note 5: 1930 census for James Twp, Stone Co, MO, has: Tony A. Hammers, 41, M21, MO, US2, Farmer, Gen Farm, with wife, Sally, 33 (??), M18, MO, OH, AR, Ora, 18, MO3, Goldie, 16, MO3, Effie, 13, MO3.

Sarah A. (Sallie) SCHWYHART and Antonio Augustus (Tony) HAMMERS were married on 4 Jan 1913 in Stone Co, MO.

Antonio Augustus (Tony) HAMMERS was born on 10 Feb 1886. He died on 20 Apr 1972.
Note1: He was buried in Philbert Cemetery, Kimberling City, Stone Co, Missouri.
Note 2: Visited gravesite, Aug 99 - Tony A. on stone
Note 3: Have put Tony with Sarah as Sally..... Aug 1999

Sarah A. (Sallie) SCHWYHART and Antonio Augustus (Tony) HAMMERS had the following children:

+42	i.	**Ora Mae HAMMERS**, born on 26 Mar 1912, Stone Co, MO; died on 9 Dec 2000, Miller, MO.
+43	ii.	**Goldie HAMMERS**, born on 24 May 1914, Stone Co, MO; died on 16 Apr 1991.
+44	iii.	**Bessie HAMMERS**, born on 29 Jun 1920.
+45	iv.	**Effie HAMMERS**, born in 1922.
+46	v.	**Mildred HAMMERS**, born on 18 Sep 1924, Stone Co, MO; died on 1 Jun 1968.
+47	vi.	**Jewel Alene (Jean) HAMMERS**, born on 7 Sep 1929.

11. **Elmer Ell SCHWYHART** (James M.-1) was born on 3 Mar 1897 in Marmaros, Stone Co, Missouri. He died on 31 Jul 1975 in Oroville, Butte Co, California.
Note 1: James Twp, Stone Co, MO, 1900 census, 3, 12 in 1910, MO, on own in 1920, age 24, with wife, Martha. Laborer, Gen Farm, in 1920.
Note 2: Birth day per Karen Nucci, Aug 1999; also, death date and place, and full names of both wives; city and county of birth.
Note 3: Per Karen Nucci information, 6 Sep 1999: more details.
Note 4: 1930 census, Oroville, Butte Co, CA, has: Almer (Elmer) L., 32, MO, with wife, Martha, 31, son, Leslie L., 14, daughter Irene V., 10, and son Robert M. 6.

Elmer Ell SCHWYHART first married Martha Jane PITTS on 17 Jan 1914 in Stone Co, Missouri.

Martha Jane PITTS (daughter of John PITTS and Naoma SMITH) was born on 7 Sep 1899 in Springfield, Missouri. She died on 19 Oct 1976 in Oroville, Butte Co, California.
Note 1: James Twp, Stone Co, MO, 1920 census, 20, MO
Note 2: Full Name per Karen Nucci, Aug 1999 (just had first from census)

Elmer Ell SCHWYHART and Martha Jane PITTS had the following children:

+48	i.	**Lester Leslie SCHWYHART**, born on 3 Jan 1916, Reed Springs, Missouri; died on 7 Sep 1990, Melborne, Florida.
+49	ii.	**Violet Irene SCHWYHART**, born on 29 Dec 1919, Radical, Missouri; married Fern Walter HENTON, on 26 Dec 1939, Carson City, Nevada; died on 2 Feb 1989, Portsmouth, Virginia.
+50	iii.	**Robert Marion SCHWYHART**, born on 31 Dec 1923, Oroville, Butte Co, California; died on 28 Apr 1997, Oroville, Butte Co, California.

Elmer Ell SCHWYHART second married Helen Anna FUSHA – additional information sought.

Helen Anna FUSHA was born on 21 Jul 1901 in Chicago, Illinois. She died on 23 Jun 1974 in Oroville, Butte Co, California.
Note 1: Name per Karen Nucci, Aug 1999.
Note 2: Per Karen Nucci sheets, 8 Sept 1999: birth and death dates and places.
Note 3: SSDI also has these dates for Helen.

Third Generation

13. **(Riley) John Riley Yocum SCHWYHART** (George Mitchell-2, James M.-1) was born on 8 May 1890 in Baxter, Stone Co, Missouri. He died on 14 Mar 1976 in Tulsa, Tulsa Co, Oklahoma.
Note 1: James Twp, Stone Co, MO, 1900 census, 10, MO
Note 2: Per Karen Nucci sheets, Sep 1999: death and marriage info
Note 3: Served in World War I.
Note 4: 1930 census for Tulsa, Tulsa Co, OK, has: John R. Schwyhart, 39, MO, with wife, Lola, 32.
Note 5: SSDI has these dates with John, last res to Tulsa, Tulsa Co.

(Riley) John Riley Yocum SCHWYHART and Lola TALIAFERRO were married on 29 Aug 1920 in Oklahoma.

Lola TALIAFERRO – more information sought.
Note 1: Per Karen Nucci sheets, Sep 1999:

14. **Matilda Alma Mary SCHWYHART** (George Mitchell-2, James M.-1) was born on 8 Apr 1893 in Baxter, Stone Co, Missouri. She died on 9 Jan 1916.
Note 1: Per Karen Nucci sheets, Sep 1999: death date and marriage date and husband name

Matilda Alma Mary SCHWYHART and William Sherman LITTLE were married on 29 Apr 1909.

William Sherman LITTLE was born in 1885 in Missouri.
Note 1: James Twp, Stone Co, MO, 1910 census, 25, MO; married once, 11/12, one child, listed.
Note 2: Per Karen Nucci sheets, Sep 1999: middle name, marriage day

Matilda Alma Mary SCHWYHART and William Sherman LITTLE had the following children:

    51   i. **Ala B. LITTLE** was born in 1910 in Missouri.
                Note 1: James Twp, Stone Co, MO, 1910 census, nr, MO

15. **James Garfield SCHWYHART** (George Mitchell-2, James M.-1) was born on 8 Feb 1895 in Baxter, Stone Co, Missouri. He died on 5 Apr 1978 in Branson, Missouri.
Note 1: Per Karen Nucci sheets, Sep 1999: death info - also says born in Gore, OK?
Note 2: SSDI has birth and death dates, also.

Florence Alta BURRIS (daughter of Newton BURRIS and Margaret CAREY) was born on 14 Dec 1898 in Stone Co, Missouri. She died on 16 Apr 1974 in Springer, New Mexico.
Note 1: Name from Karen Nucci, Aug 1999.
Note 2: Per Karen Nucci sheets, 8 Sept 1999: also had birth and death date and place - had 10 children - I had eight - names only, both.

James Garfield SCHWYHART and Florence Alta BURRIS had the following children:

52   i.   **James Richard SCHWYHART** was born on 23 Jun 1925. He died in Oct 1977.
Note 1: At Ancestry.com, 26 Apr 2005.
Note 2: Last Social Security Check to Kansas City, MO 64106
Note 3: James G. Schwyhart obit, 20 Apr 1978 newspaper, Galena, Stone Co, MO: James, Stockton, CA
Note 4: Per Karen Nucci sheets, 8 Sept 1999: middle name

+53   ii.   **George Washington SCHWYHART**, born on 24 Sep 1926; married Loretta F. GIDEON.
Note 1: People Search by Nancy.

54   iii.   **Bill Joe SCHWYHART**
Note 1: James G. Schwyhart obit, 20 Apr 1978 newspaper, Galena, Stone Co, MO: Bill, Springfield.
Note 2: Per Karen Nucci sheets, 8 Sept 1999: middle name.

+55   iv.   **Wilma Lee SCHWYHART**, married Stanley Glenn HARPER.

56   v.   **Lula Mae SCHWYHART**
Note 1: James G. Schwyhart obit, 20 Apr 1978 newspaper, Galena, Stone Co, MO: Mrs. Lula Thomas, Stockton, CA
Note 2: Per Karen Nucci sheets, 8 Sept 1999: middle name

57   vi.   **Nadine SCHWYHART**
Note 1: James G. Schwyhart obit, 20 Apr 1978 newspaper, Galena, Stone Co, MO: Mrs. Nadine Tirapelle, Stockton, CA

58   vii.   **Florence SCHWYHART**
Note 1: James G. Schwyhart obit, 20 Apr 1978 newspaper, Galena, Stone Co, MO: Mrs. Florence Milam, Manning, S.C.

59   viii.   **Clifford Martin SCHWYHART**
Note 1: Per Karen Nucci sheets, 8 Sept 1999: name

+60   ix.   **Frances Margaret SCHWYHART**, born on 21 May 1925, Baxter, Stone Co, Missouri; married Franklin Henry BRAY, on 25 Jul 1952; died on 25 Jul 1970.
Note 1: IGI on Family Search.com
Note 2: Elvin Haynes email June 2006
Note 3: IGI on Family Search.com

61   x.   **Alta Ruth SCHWYHART** was born.
Note 1: Per Karen Nucci sheets, 8 Sept 1999: name

16. **Joseph Lincoln SCHWYHART** (George Mitchell-2, James M.-1) was born on 8 Mar 1897 in Baxter, Stone Co, Missouri. He died on 24 Mar 1985 in Springfield, Missouri. He was buried in Kimberling City, Missouri.
Note 1: James G. Schwyhart obit, 20 Apr 1978 newspaper, Galena, Stone Co, MO: Joe listed as surviving brother, Lampe.
Note 2: His obit in 28 Mar 1985 Crane Chronicle/Stone County (MO) Republican. Joseph is survived by wife, Irene, and two sons, Joe L. and Bean; six grandchildren and five g-great grandchildren.

Note 3: Per Karen Nucci sheets, Sep 1999: death info
Note 4: SSDI has these birth and death dates, with Joe.

Joseph Lincoln SCHWYHART and Irene HARGROVE were married on 4 Mar 1941 in Berryville, Carroll Co, Arkansas.

Irene HARGROVE was born on 25 Jan 1915 in Baxter, Stone Co, Missouri.
Note 1: Husband's obit
Note 2: Per Karen Nucci sheets, 8 Sept 1999: last name, birth date and place.

Joseph Lincoln SCHWYHART and Irene HARGROVE had the following children:

62	i.	**Joseph Leroy (Joe) SCHWYHART** was born on 11 Sep 1931. He died on 11 Aug 1987 in St.John's Regional HC, Missouri. He was buried on 14 Aug 1987 in Philbert Cemetery, Kimberling City, Stone Co, Missouri.

Note 1: Obit 1987, from Galena Library, Stone Co, MO
Note 2: http://www.fraudulenttransfers.com/1996_MO_22642.htm (Google Search, 26 Apr 2005) new on lawsuit.

63	ii.	**Carthel Dean SCHWYHART** was born.

Note 1: Joseph Schwyhart obit, 28 Mar 1985 Crane Chronicle/Stone County Republican, Galena Library, Stone Co, MO: had Bean!
Note 2: Per Karen Nucci sheets, 8 Sept 1999: Carthel Dean!

17. **William Aster SCHWYHART** (George Mitchell-2, James M.-1) was born on 2 Oct 1899 in Baxter, Stone Co, Missouri. He died in Jul 1973 in Skaggs Hosp, Branson, Taney Co, Missouri. He was buried in Philbert Cemetery, Kimberling City, Stone Co, Missouri.
Note 1: S.S. Death report and obit from Stone Co, Galena Library, MO, Aug 1999
Note 2: Per Karen Nucci sheets, Sep 1999: middle name - she has 7 Sep death date??
Note 3: SSDI confirms birth and death dates.

William Aster SCHWYHART and Josie Bell YOKUM were married on 9 Jul 1927 in Berryville, Carroll Co, Arkansas.

Josie Bell YOKUM was born on 16 Feb 1905. She died on 10 Dec 1994. She was buried in Philbert Cemetery, Kimberling City, Stone Co, Missouri.
Note 1: Husband's obit
Note 2: Birth date and death date from both her stone and S.S. Death info
Note 3: Per Karen Nucci sheets, 8 Sept 1999: middle and last name.
Note 4: SSDI has same birth and death dates.

William Aster SCHWYHART and Josie Bell YOKUM had the following children:

+64	i.	**Kendall Ray SCHWYHART**, born on 15 Mar 1943; died on 21 Mar 1987, Lampe, Stone Co, Missouri.

18. **Ceanith Anita SCHWYHART** (George Mitchell-2, James M.-1) was born on 22 Feb 1903 in Baxter, Stone Co, Missouri.

Note 1: James Twp, Stone Co, MO, 1910 census, 7, MO: Oveta A.
Note 2: Per Karen Nucci sheets, Sep 1999: Ceanith Anita, birth date and place, husband

Ceanith Amita SCHWYHART married Joe AUSTIN – more information sought.

Joe AUSTIN – more information sought.
Note 1: Per Karen Nucci sheets, Sep 1999: Name

19. **Helen Agnes SCHWYHART** (George Mitchell-2, James M.-1) was born on 26 Sep 1906 in Baxter, Stone Co, Missouri. She died on 26 Jul 1976 in Pocatello, Bannock Co, Idaho. She was buried in Pocatello, Bannock Co, Idaho.
Note 1: Per Karen Nucci sheets, Sep 1999: death info
Note 2: Death and Burial Per B. Pitts Sheets, Sep 99.

Helen Agnes SCHWYHART second married (Tony) Charles Edward Antonie PITTS on 5 Oct 1940 in Forsyth, Taney Co, Missouri.

(Tony) Charles Edward Antonie PITTS was born on 3 Sep 1910 in Baxter, Stone Co, Missouri. He died on 5 Nov 1970 in Lampe, Stone Co, Missouri. He was buried on 10 Nov 1970 in Kimberling Cemetery, Stone Co, Missouri.
Note 1: Per Jean Sherwood email, Jun 1999
Note 2: Tony full name from Karen Nucci, Aug 1999
Note 3: Per Karen Nucci sheets, 8 Sept 1999: birth date and place added
Note 4: Death information per B. Pitts Sheets, Sep 99.

Helen Agnes SCHWYHART and (Tony) Charles Edward Antonie PITTS had the following children:

+65   i. **Bernard Ray PITTS**, born on 16 Jun 1944, Lampe, Stone Co, Missouri; married Tua Emmeline KATTER, on 30 Dec 1970, Oakland, Alameda Co, California.

Helen Agnes SCHWYHART first married Leuvoka Lee HARGROVE on 26 Mar 1925 in Baxter, Stone Co, Missouri.

Leuvoka Lee HARGROVE was born on 7 Dec 1887 in Billings, Christian Co, Missouri. He died on 2 Oct 1938 in Springfield, Missouri.
Note 1: Name per Karen Nucci, Aug 1999.
Note 2: Per Karen Nucci sheets, 8 Sept 1999: Birth and death dates and places.

Helen Agnes SCHWYHART and Leuvoka Lee HARGROVE had the following children:

+66   i. **Mildred HARGROVE**, born on 19 Jul 1925, Lampe, Stone Co, Missouri.
+67   ii. **Margarie HARGROVE**, born on 3 Oct 1926, Lampe, Stone Co, Missouri; married Marvin Vernon GRAY, on 31 Oct 1942, Galena, Stone Co, Missouri.

+68	iii.	**Lula HARGROVE**, born on 31 Mar 1933, Lampe, Stone Co, Missouri; married Richard Allen STEPHENS, on 5 Jun 1949, Oroville, Butte Co, California.
+69	iv.	**Lee HARGROVE**, born on 6 Sep 1934, Lampe, Stone Co, Missouri.

24. **Ethel GORE** (Jeanette (Nettie) (Jennie) SCHWYHART-2, James M.-1) was born in 1906 in Missouri.
Note 1: James Twp, Stone Co, MO, 1920 census, 14, MO

Ethel GORE married Unknown NIX – more information sought.

UNKNOWN NIX – more information sought.

Ethel GORE and NIX had the following children:

+70	i.	**Beulah NIX**.
+71	ii.	**Vivian Bernice (Bernice) NIX**, born on 16 Jan 1939, Haskel County, Oklahoma; married Elmer Ralph (Sam) HUFF, on 13 Mar 1954, Reno, Washoe Co, Nevada.

28. **Stella GORE** (Jeanette (Nettie) (Jennie) SCHWYHART-2, James M.-1) was born in 1916 in Missouri.
Note 1: James Twp, Stone Co, MO, 1920 census, 3 11/12, MO

Stella GORE married Unknown SHAW – more information sought.

UNKNOWN SHAW – more information sought.

34. **Isaac William (Ike) SCHWYHART** (William Robert-2, James M.-1) was born on 17 Dec 1921. He died on 7 Aug 2003 in Cedarville, Modoc Co, CA.
Note 1: Per Karen Nucci sheets, Sep 1999: name and birth date
Note 2: SSDI has Isaac W Schwyhart, b. 17 Dec 1921, d. 7 Aug 2003, Cedarville, Modoc, CA, issues OR.

Isaac William (Ike) SCHWYHART and Betty MADISON were married on 1 Jan 1948.

Betty MADISON was born on 23 Mar 1923. She died on 15 Mar 1994 in Cedarville, Modoc Co, CA.
Note 1: Per Karen Nucci sheets, 8 Sept 1999:
Note 2: SSDI has Betty A. Schwyhart, b.23 Mar 1923, d. 15 Mar 1994, Cedarville, Modoc Co, CA, issued IL.

Isaac William (Ike) SCHWYHART and Betty MADISON had the following children:

72	i.	**Joanne SCHWYHART**
		Note 1: Per Karen Nucci sheets, 8 Sept 1999: name

73	ii.	**Dale SCHWYHART**
		Note 1: Per Karen Nucci sheets, 8 Sept 1999: name
74	iii.	**Bob SCHWYHART**
		Note 1: Per Karen Nucci sheets, 8 Sept 1999: name

35. **James Old (Jim) SCHWYHART** (William Robert-2, James M.-1) was born on 13 Jun 1925. He died on 25 Oct 1977.
Note 1: Per Julie 2 Oct 99 email update: additional children on William Robert and Annie Alley.
Note 2: SSDI has birth date and death date, also.
Note 3: Old not Owd, per daughter-in-law Rose Mar 08

James Old (Jim) SCHWYHART married Donna BARRY – more information sought

Donna BARRY – more information sought.
Note 1: Per Julie 2 Oct 99 email update: additional children on William Robert and Annie Alley.

James Old (Jim) SCHWYHART and Donna BARRY had the following children:

+75	i.	**William (Billy) SCHWYHART**, married Rose VILLANUEVA, in 1985.
76	ii.	**Sheryl SCHWYHART** was born.
		Note 1: Per Julie 2 Oct 99 email update: additional children on William Robert and Annie Alley.
77	iii.	**Barbara Ann SCHWYHART** was born.
		Note 1: Per Julie 2 Oct 99 email update: additional children on William Robert and Annie Alley.

36. **Lizzie R. SCHWYHART** (William Robert-2, James M.-1) was born on 16 Jul 1929.
Note 1: Per Julie 2 Oct 99 email update: additional children on William Robert and Annie Alley.
Note 2: Living in Hollister, MO.

Lizzie R. SCHWYHART first married Ralph COX – more information sought.

Ralph COX
Note 1: Per Julie 2 Oct 99 email update: additional children on William Robert and Annie Alley.

Lizzie R. SCHWYHART and Ralph COX had the following children:

| 78 | i. | **Michael COX** was born. |
| | | Note 1: Per Julie 2 Oct 99 email update: additional children on William Robert and Annie Alley. |

Lizzie R. SCHWYHART second married Riley CLIFT – more information sought

Riley CLIFT – additional information sought.
Note 1: Per Julie 2 Oct 99 email update: additional children on William Robert and Annie Alley.

37. **John SCHWYHART** (William Robert-2, James M.-1) was born on 18 Dec 1931. He died

on 2 Dec 1985. He was buried in McCarty Cemetery, Taney Co, Missouri.
Note 1: Per Karen Nucci sheets, Sep 1999: name and birthdate
Note 2: Cemetery info - also has Pfc US Army Korea.
Note 3: Per Julie 2 Oct 99 email update: additional children on William Robert and Annie Alley: death date confirmed plus wife and children info
Note 4: SSDI also has these birth and death dates.

John SCHWYHART married Kathy WILLENBERG – more information sought.

Kathy WILLENBERG – more information sought.
Note 1: Per Julie 2 Oct 99 email update: additional children on William Robert and Annie Alley.
Note 2: Last name spelling in question.

John SCHWYHART and Kathy WILLENBERG had the following children:

79	i.	**Kirsten SCHWYHART**
		Note 1: Per Julie 2 Oct 99 email update: additional children on William Robert and Annie Alley.
80	ii.	**Linda SCHWYHART**
		Note 1: Per Julie 2 Oct 99 email update: additional children on William Robert and Annie Alley.
81	iii.	**Shawneree SCHWYHART**
		Note 1: Per Julie 2 Oct 99 email update: additional children on William Robert and Annie Alley.
82	iv.	**John SCHWYHART**
		Note 1: Per Julie 2 Oct 99 email update: additional children on William Robert and Annie Alley.

38. **Gene Ray SCHWYHART** (William Robert-2, James M.-1) was born on 5 Oct 1934.
Note 1: Per Karen Nucci sheets, Sep 1999: name and name of wife
Note 2: Birth date per Juli
Note 3: Per Julie 2 Oct 99 email update: additional children on William Robert and Annie Alley. - wife and children info

Gene Ray SCHWYHART married Jewel GOODALL – more information sought.

Jewel GOODALL – more information sought.
Note 1: Per Juli

Gene Ray SCHWYHART and Jewel GOODALL had the following children:

+83	i.	**Bradley Eugene SCHWYHART**, born on 20 Oct 1968, Branson, Taney Co, Missouri.
+84	ii.	**Brady William SCHWYHART**, born on 25 Aug 1970; married Julia Ann (Juli) JONES, on 18 Sep 1994.
85	iii.	**Paula Marie SCHWYHART** was born on 15 Mar 1985 in Branson, Taney Co, Missouri.

Note 1: Per Julie 2 Oct 99 email update: additional children on William Robert and Annie Alley.

39. Nora SCHWYHART (William Robert-2, James M.-1) was born on 26 Mar 1937.
Note 1: Per Julie 2 Oct 99 email update: additional children on William Robert and Annie Alley.
Note 2: Living in Warsaw, MO

Nora SCHWYHART married Thurman MARLER – more information sought.

Thurman MARLER – more information sought.
Note 1: Per Julie 2 Oct 99 email update: additional children on William Robert and Annie Alley.

Nora SCHWYHART and Thurman MARLER had the following children:

86	i.	**Patty Ann MARLER**

Note 1: Per Julie 2 Oct 99 email update: additional children on William Robert and Annie Alley.

87	ii.	**Robert William MARLER**

Note 1: Per Julie 2 Oct 99 email update: additional children on William Robert and Annie Alley.

40. Mary SCHWYHART (William Robert-2, James M.-1) was born on 25 Dec 1939.
Note 1: Per Karen Nucci sheets, Sep 1999: name and name of husband
Note 2: Per Julie 2 Oct 99 email update: additional children on William Robert and Annie Alley.

Mary SCHWYHART married Dean JONES – more information sought.

Dean JONES – more information sought.
Note 1: Per Juli

41. Bobby J. SCHWYHART (William Robert-2, James M.-1) was born in 1944/45. He died on 14 Apr 2004 in St. Louis, Missouri.
Note 1: Per Karen Nucci sheets, Sep 1999: name
Note 2: Per Julie 2 Oct 99 email update: additional children on William Robert and Annie Alley.
Note 3: Birth year est. and wife and children info

Bobby J. SCHWYHART married Jeanette WILLENBERG – more information sought.

Jeanette WILLENBERG – more information sought.
Note 1: Per Julie 2 Oct 99 email update: additional children on William Robert and Annie Alley.
Note 2: Spelling a question.
Note 3: Sister to Kathy, married to John, brother of Bobby.

Bobby J. SCHWYHART and Jeanette WILLENBERG had the following children:

88	i.	**Kenneth SCHWYHART**

Note 1: Per Julie 2 Oct 99 email update: additional children on William Robert and Annie Alley.

+89   ii. **Kimberly SCHWYHART**.

42. **Ora Mae HAMMERS** (Sarah A. (Sallie) SCHWYHART-2, James M.-1) was born on 26 Mar 1912 in Stone Co, MO. He died on 9 Dec 2000 in Miller, MO.
Note 1: Per Karen Nucci sheets, 8 Sept 1999:
Note 2: Married twice, to Tice Freeman and Macklin Orr.

Ora Mae HAMEERS first married Clarence Edward (Tice) FREEMAN – more information sought.

Clarence Edward (Tice) FREEMAN – more information sought.

Ora Mae HAMEERS second married Macklin ORR – more information sought.

Macklin ORR – more information sought.

43. **Goldie HAMMERS** (Sarah A. (Sallie) SCHWYHART-2, James M.-1) was born on 24 May 1914 in Stone Co, MO. She died on 16 Apr 1991.
Note 1: Per Karen Nucci sheets, 8 Sept 1999:
Note 2: Goldie married to Charles David Town.
Note 3: She had a daughter, Norma, who married Victor Tompkin.

Goldie HAMMERS married Charles David TOWN – more information sought.

Charles David TOWN

Goldie HAMMERS and Charles David TOWN had the following children:

+90   i. **Norma TOWN**

44. **Bessie HAMMERS** (Sarah A. (Sallie) SCHWYHART-2, James M.-1) was born on 29 Jun 1920.
Note 1: Per Karen Nucci sheets, 8 Sept 1999:

Bessie HAMMERS married William Thomas (Punk) CAMPBELL – more information sought.

William Thomas (Punk) CAMPBELL was born on 12 Feb 1923. He died on 7 Jun 1993 in Stotts City, Lawrence Co, MO.
Note 1: SSDI has William T. Campbell: b. 12 Feb 1923; 7 Jun 1993; last res: 65756, Stotts City, Lawrence Co, MO.

45. **Effie HAMMERS** (Sarah A. (Sallie) SCHWYHART-2, James M.-1) was born in 1922.

Note 1: Per Karen Nucci sheets, 8 Sept 1999:

Effie HAMMERS first married George DAVIS – more information sought.

George DAVIS died on 20 Aug 1962.

Effie HAMMERS second married A. J. BONNER – more information sought.

A. L. BONNER – more information sought.
Note 1: Effie's 2nd husband.

Effie HAMMERS and A. L. BONNER had the following children:

+91   i.   **Violet BONNER**, died on 10 May 1993.

46. **Mildred HAMMERS** (Sarah A. (Sallie) SCHWYHART-2, James M.-1) was born on 18 Sep 1924 in Stone Co, MO. She died on 1 Jun 1968.
Note 1: Per Karen Nucci sheets, 8 Sept 1999.
Note 2: When Mildred died, her sister Jean married Donald Janes and Jean adopted Mildred's children by Mr. Janes as well as Ted Davis.

Mildred HAMMERS first married Ralph WILSON – more information sought.

Ralph WILSON – more information sought.
Note 1: Mildred's first husband.

Mildred HAMMERS and Ralph WILSON had the following children:

92   i.   **Richard WILSON**
93   ii. **Helen WILSON**
94   iii. **Bonnie WILSON**

Mildred HAMMERS second married Lloyd MOORE – more information sought.

Lloyd MOORE – more information sought.
Note 1: Mildred's 2nd husband.

Mildred HAMMERS third married Ted DAVIS – more information sought.

Ted DAVIS – more information sought.
Note 1: Mildred's 3rd husband.

Mildred HAMMERS and Ted DAVIS had the following children:

95   i.   **Robert Ted DAVIS JANES** was born.
                 Note 1: Son of Mildred and Ted Davis. He was adopted by Jean and Don Janes and took the name Janes.

Mildred HAMMERS fourth married Donald Richard JANES.

Donald Richard JANES was born on 26 May 1920. He died on 10 Jan 1996 in Seligman, Barry Co, MO.
Note 1: Mildred's 4th husband.
Note 2: Jean's 3rd husband.
Note 3: SSDI has Donald R. Janes, last res: 65745, Seligman, Barry Co, MO; b. 26 May 1920; d. 10 Jan 1996.

Mildred HAMMERS and Donald Richard JANES had the following children:

96	i.	**Anthony JANES**
97	ii.	**Rebecca JANES**
98	iii.	**Ruth Ellen JANES**
99	iv.	**Michael JANES**
100	v.	**Elizabeth JANES**

47. **Jewel Alene (Jean) HAMMERS** (Sarah A. (Sallie) SCHWYHART-2, James M.-1) was born on 7 Sep 1929.
Note 1: Per Karen Nucci sheets, 8 Sept 1999:
Note 2: After her second husband was gone (died, perhaps), her older sister, Mildred, died. Their father encouraged Jean to 'go out with' Donald James, Mildred's widower husband. She wasn't too excited about it, but was worried about the children. They ultimately married and were very happy. Jean raised 11 children: 5 of her own and 6 of Mildred's.
Note 3: After raising 11 children, she has also managed to be a woman of note in Seligman. She has been the dispatcher for the Fire Dept. since 1979 and reportedly has done wonders for it's ASO ratings due to her good record keeping, was Seligman's first Woman Mayor in 1988 and 1989, has been on the City Council and worked the Election Polls since 1986. Was founder of the Seligman Senior Citizen's Organization, has been Secretary-Treasurer for the Coon Hunters since 1976 and was the first woman in the Seligman Lions Club and also on the City Park Board.

Jewel Alene (Jean) HAMMERS first married Clarence Vancil CRON – more information sought.

Clarence Vancil CRON– more information sought.
Note 1: Clarence and Jean divorced.

Jewel Alene (Jean) HAMMERS and Clarence Vancil CRON had the following children:

101	i.	**Carol CRON**– more information sought.

Jewel Alene (Jean) HAMMERS second married Roy (Rod) WHITE – more information sought.

Roy (Rod) WHITE– more information sought.
Note 1: He died...about time that Jean's sister, Mildred, died...

Jewel Alene (Jean) HAMMERS third married Donald Richard JANES – more information sought.

Donald Richard JANES was born on 26 May 1920. He died on 10 Jan 1996 in Seligman, Barry Co, MO.
Note 1: Mildred's 4th husband.
Note 2: Jean's 3rd husband.
Note 3: SSDI has Donald R. Janes, last res: 65745, Seligman, Barry Co, MO; b. 26 May 1920; d. 10 Jan 1996.

48. **Lester Leslie SCHWYHART** (Elmer Ell-2, James M.-1) was born on 3 Jan 1916 in Reed Springs, Missouri. He died on 7 Sep 1990 in Melborne, Florida.
Note 1: James Twp, Stone Co, MO, 1920 census, 3 4/12, MO
Note 2: Per Karen Nucci sheets, 8 Sept 1999: birth and date details.
Note 3: Dates also on SSDI, Issued RR before 1951.

Lester Leslie SCHWYHART married Oleva CROSS – more information sought.

Oleva CROSS was born on 6 Aug 1917 in Colorado. She died on 9 May 1990 in Oroville, Butte Co, California.
Note 1: Per Karen Nucci sheets, 8 Sept 1999:

Lester Leslie SCHWYHART and Oleva CROSS had the following children:

+102   i. **Sue Ann SCHWYHART**, born on 3 Jun 1946; married Tom HASENMYER, on 11 Oct 1968, Reno, Nevada.

49. **Violet Irene SCHWYHART** (Elmer Ell-2, James M.-1) was born on 29 Dec 1919 in Radical, Missouri. She died on 2 Feb 1989 in Portsmouth, Virginia.
Note 1: James Twp, Stone Co, MO, 1900 census, 0/12, MO
Note 2: Per Karen Nucci sheets, 8 Sept 1999: birth and death details.

Violet Irene SCHWYHART and Fern Walter HENTON were married on 26 Dec 1939 in Carson City, Nevada.

Fern Walter HENTON was born on 13 Apr 1920 in White Sulphur Springs, Montana. He died on 4 Jun 1982 in Alameda, Alameda Co, California.
Note 1: Per Karen Nucci sheets, 8 Sept 1999

Violet Irene SCHWYHART and Fern Walter HENTON had the following children:

103   i. **Wallace Frederick HENTON** was born on 11 Nov 1943 in Oroville, Butte Co, California. He died on 11 Nov 1943 in Oroville, Butte Co, California.
      Note 1: Per Karen Nucci sheets, 8 Sept 1999:
+104   ii. **Karen Jane HENTON**, born on 9 Sep 1946, San Mateo, California; married George NUCCI, on 1 May 1965, Alameda, Alameda Co, California.
105   iii. **Kathy HENTON** was born on 20 Jul 1954 in Sacramento, California. She

died on 21 Jul 1954 in Sacramento, California.
Note 1: Per Karen Nucci sheets, 8 Sept 1999:

50. **Robert Marion SCHWYHART** (Elmer Ell-2, James M.-1) was born on 31 Dec 1923 in Oroville, Butte Co, California. He died on 28 Apr 1997 in Oroville, Butte Co, California.
Note 1: Per Karen Nucci sheets, 8 Sept 1999: name and birth and death details.
Note 2: SSDI confirms birth and death dates.

Robert Marion SCHWYHART married Zadell SCHAUER – more information sought.

Zadell SCHAUER was born on 30 Dec 1924 in San Jose, California. She died on 11 Mar 1996 in Oroville, Butte Co, California.
Note 1: Per Karen Nucci sheets, 8 Sept 1999

Robert Marion SCHWYHART and Zadell SCHAUER had the following children:

+106   i. **Robert Michael SCHWYHART**, born on 5 Sep 1945, Oakland, California; married Jeanette PILE, on 19 Dec 1964, Treasure Island, California.

Chapter 10

Isaac SCHWYHART and His Descendants

First Generation

1. **Isaac SCHWYHART** was born on 15 Jul 1829 in Belmont Co, Ohio. He died on 27 May 1862 in Camp Shiloh.
Note 1: Per LDS Ancestoral File
Note 2: Marriage date per e-mail note 30 Jul 1977 from Bernadine Myers via Cris Reed.
Note 3: Placement in Jacob and Sarah family Per Karen Nucci info 6 Sep 1999.
Note 4: 1860 census has Isaac, Sarah, Elizabeth, Isabel, Leann, Levinia, Mary
Note 5: Isaac military records from National Archives, shows Company H, 78 Ohio Infantry, Private.
Note 6: 5 Company Muster Roll cards on record, and 3 other cards. Four of the cards state, in various ways, that Isaac died at Camp Shiloh, 27 May 1862, of disease, Camp Fever. He enlisted on 10 December 1861, at Birmingham, OH. He was a farmer, 6 feet 1 inch in Height, Age 33, Eyes: Blue, Hair: Brown, Complexion: Dark. Also, extensive Pension File from National Archives.

Isaac SCHWYHART and Sarah Ann KIMBLE were married on 12 Sep 1850.

Sarah Ann KIMBLE was born in 1827 in Ohio.
Note 1: Village of Salem, Liberty Twp, Guernsey Co, 1870 census: 43, with 7 daughters.
Note 2: On 4 May 1867, Sarah filed a Widow's Claim for increase in Pension on behalf of herself and her listed 5 daughters: Isabella, Lee Ann, Lamira, Mary and Lydia. Sarah was of Millnersville, Liberty Twp, Guernsey Co, OH.
Note 3: On 30 Apr 1867 an affidavit was file by Sarah Kimble and Thomas McKee, stating that the 5 mentioned daughters above noted are 'the only legitimate children now living of Isaac Schwyhart, deceased, that were under sixteen years of age July 25, 1866.'
Note 4: Date of marriage on original pension application, also. Elizabeth was born two years before, so not of this marriage, since born before marriage date by two years.
Note 5: On a 12 Dec 1867 court document, related to clarifying the name of her youngest daughter on pension claim forms (Lydia M. vs. Margaret!) the following describes Sarah, 'She is a person who has no education cannot even write her own name, that she is & was compelled to depend upon others in making up a statement of the names & dates of birth, or ages, of her children...' She signed the statement with her mark.

Isaac SCHWYHART and Sarah Ann KIMBLE had the following children:

2   i.   **Elizabeth SCHWYHART** was born in 1848 in Ohio.
                Note 1: Village of Salem, Liberty Twp, Guernsey Co, 1870 census: 22, OH - assumed to be daughter, but, may be "servant" - assisting with children.
                Note 2: Need to re-read Pension files, regarding this possibility. Would have

been over 16 in 1867 when papers filed, therefore, not included?!?!?

+3	ii.	**Isabella SCHWYHART**, born on 28 Feb 1851, Guernsey Co, Ohio; married Oceola R. JONES, on 19 Oct 1874, Guernsey Co, Ohio.
4	iii.	**Lee Ann SCHWYHART** was born on 8 Sep 1852 in Guernsey Co, Ohio. Village of Salem, Liberty Twp, Guernsey Co, 1870 census: Ann, 17, OH
5	iv.	**La Mira (Elmira) SCHWYHART** was born on 18 Oct 1856 in Guernsey Co, Ohio. Note 1: Village of Salem, Liberty Twp, Guernsey Co, 1870 census: Lamira, 16, OH
+6	v.	**Mary A. SCHWYHART**, born on 20 Mar 1858, Guernsey Co, Ohio; married Alexander JONES, on 22 Jul 1874, Guernsey Co, Ohio.
7	vi.	**Lydia M. (Margaret) SCHWYHART** was born on 11 Sep 1860 in Ohio. Village of Salem, Liberty Twp, Guernsey Co, 1870 census: Margaret, 9, OH Note 1: Mother's affidavit in pension file states she was always called Margaret at home.
8	vii.	**Ellen O. SCHWYHART** was born in 1867 in Ohio. Note 1: Village of Salem, Liberty Twp, Guernsey Co, 1870 census: Ellen O., 3, OH. Not a daughter of Isaac, since he died at Shiloh in 1863.....

Second Generation

3. **Isabella SCHWYHART** (Isaac-1) was born on 28 Feb 1851 in Guernsey Co, Ohio.
Note 1: Per LDS Ancestoral File
Note 2: Village of Salem, Liberty Twp, Guernsey Co, 1870 census: 19, OH

Isabella SCHWYHART and Oceola R. JONES were married on 19 Oct 1874 in Guernsey Co, Ohio.

Oceola R. JONES (son of James L. JONES and Louisa DAWSON) was born in 1855 in Ohio. He died in 1924 in Guernsey Co, Ohio. He was buried in North Salem C. Church Cemetery.
Note 1: Ancestry World Tree - Family Information: Parents James L. Jones and Louisa Dawson
Note 2: Has no children listed for Oceloa and Isabella.

6. **Mary A. SCHWYHART** (Isaac-1) was born on 20 Mar 1858 in Guernsey Co, Ohio.
Village of Salem, Liberty Twp, Guernsey Co, 1870 census: Mary, 13, OH

Mary A. SCHWYHART and Alexander JONES were married on 22 Jul 1874 in Guernsey Co, Ohio.

Alexander JONES (son of James L. JONES and Louisa DAWSON) was born on 3 Jul 1852 in Ohio. He was buried in Muskingum Co, Ohio.
Note 1: Bernadine Myers chart of 1984.
Note 2: Alexander and his 1st wife, Adaline Maffit, had a child, Austin B. Jones, 5 May 1873.

Mary A. SCHWYHART and Alexander JONES had the following children:

9	i.	**Isaac Lori JONES** was born on 17 May 1875 in Liberty Twp, Guernsey Co, Ohio. Note 1: 1st wife, Edith Mohler, died six months after her marriage. Thelma Sebaugh Jones, daughter of Isaac (Lori) and his 2nd wife, Lena.
10	ii.	**Sarah Moreley JONES** was born on 22 Nov 1877 in Wheeling Twp, Guernsey Co, Ohio. She died on 28 May 1885 in North Salem, Guernsey Co, Ohio. She was buried in Bells Cemetery.
11	iii.	**Clifford E. JONES** was born on 17 May 1879 in Ohio. Note 1: Clifford killed on motorcycle.
12	iv.	**David F. JONES** was born on 15 Feb 1881 in Ohio.
+13	v.	**Perley Russell JONES**, born on 5 Jul 1883, Guernsey Co, Ohio; married Ollie May PARKINSON, on 28 Jul 1904, Zanesville, Muskingum Co, Ohio.
14	vi.	**James B. JONES** was born on 21 Apr 1885 in Liberty Twp, Guernsey Co, Ohio. He died on 10 Jan 1886.
+15	vii.	**John Logan JONES**, born on 21 Apr 1885, Liberty Twp, Guernsey Co, Ohio; married Cora LUGSBY, on 25 Jul 1906, Muskingum Co, Ohio.
+16	viii.	**Lamira S. JONES**, born on 2 Apr 1887, Ohio.
17	ix.	**Harry Curtis JONES** was born on 20 May 1889 in Ohio.
+18	x.	**Ethel Bell JONES**, born on 17 Apr 1891, Ohio.
19	xi.	**Erna JONES** was born on 20 Feb 1893. She died on 27 Jun 1893.
20	xii.	**Edwin JONES** was born on 20 Feb 1893. He died on 9 Jul 1893 in Zanesville, Muskingum Co, Ohio.
21	xiii.	**Edna JONES** was born on 20 Feb 1893. She died on 9 Aug 1893.
+22	xiv.	**Edith D. JONES**, born on 7 Apr 1895, Ohio; married James MELVEN, Columbus.
23	xv.	**Chester M. JONES** was born on 18 Jan 1899. He died on 17 Dec 1899.
+24	xvi.	**Oscar B. JONES**, born on 27 Aug 1901; married Unknown, Texas; died in Jun 1961.

Third Generation

13. **Perley Russell JONES** (Mary A. SCHWYHART-2, Isaac-1) was born on 5 Jul 1883 in Guernsey Co, Ohio.
Note 1: Bernadine Myers chart of 1984.
Note 2: Occupation: Coal miner.

Perley Russell JONES and Ollie May PARKINSON were married on 28 Jul 1904 in Zanesville, Muskingum Co, Ohio.

Ollie May PARKINSON (daughter of Edward PARKINSON and Arminta HANKINSON) was born on 6 Oct 1888 in Muskingum Co, Ohio. She died on 26 Feb 1936 in Muskingum Co, Ohio.
Note 1: Bernadine Myers chart of 1984

Perley Russell JONES and Ollie May PARKINSON had the following children:

25	i.	**Perley Russell JONES** was born on 13 Jun 1906. He died on 13 Jun 1906.
+26	ii.	**Ernest James JONES**, born on 9 Aug 1907, Zanesville, Muskingum Co, Ohio; married Mildred Mae HOLDCROFT, on 26 Nov 1927, Zanesville, Muskingum Co, Ohio; died on 30 Nov 1964, Wellston, Missouri.
+27	iii.	**Ruth D. JONES**, born on 13 May 1909; died on 24 May 1960, Hawkins, WI.
+28	iv.	**Florian Frances JONES**, born on 15 Nov 1910; died on 26 Nov 1969.
29	v.	**Edgar E. JONES** was born on 10 Jan 1913. He died on 2 Jan 1920.
+30	vi.	**Beatrice M. JONES**, born on 22 Sep 1915; died on 19 Aug 1956, Zanesville, Muskingum Co, Ohio.
+31	vii.	**Helen J. JONES**, born on 22 May 1917; died on 7 Oct 1970, Zanesville, Muskingum Co, Ohio.
32	viii.	**Clifford L. JONES** was born on 24 Jul 1919. He died on 2 Mar 1920.
+33	ix.	**Walter Dale JONES**, born on 2 Jan 1922.
34	x.	**Harry Curtis JONES** was born on 20 Apr 1924. He died on 5 Oct 1970.

15. **John Logan JONES** (Mary A. SCHWYHART-2, Isaac-1) was born on 21 Apr 1885 in Liberty Twp, Guernsey Co, Ohio.

John Logan JONES and Cora LUGSBY were married on 25 Jul 1906 in Muskingum Co, Ohio.

Cora LUGSBY – more information sought.

16. **Lamira S. JONES** (Mary A. SCHWYHART-2, Isaac-1) was born on 2 Apr 1887 in Ohio.

Lamira S. JONES married Charles Carl BUMBAUGH – more information sought.

Charles Carl BUMBAUGH – more information sought.

18. **Ethel Bell JONES** (Mary A. SCHWYHART-2, Isaac-1) was born on 17 Apr 1891 in Ohio. She was buried in Greenwood Cemetery.

Ethel Bell JONES married Earl KINNEY – more information sought.

Earl KINNEY - more information sought.

22. **Edith D. JONES** (Mary A. SCHWYHART-2, Isaac-1) was born on 7 Apr 1895 in Ohio.

Edith D. JONES and James MELVEN were married in Columbus.

James MELVEN – more information sought.

24. **Oscar B. JONES** (Mary A. SCHWYHART-2, Isaac-1) was born on 27 Aug 1901. He died in Jun 1961.
Note 1: Death date from SSDI, issued Texas, last res/last benefit not listed; birth date correct.

Oscar B. JONES and Unknown UNKNOWN were married in Texas.

Unknown UNKNOWN – more information sought.

Acknowledgements and List of Contributors

First, let me recognize the contributions of all those folks with whom I have chatted about this family or exchanged information that are not listed below. Thank you each for your contribution.

I also do not have a complete list of the many county offices and local historical societies and genealogical societies we have either personally visited or had correspondence with over the past fifteen plus years. Some of them are mentioned in the text, in notes, but not all, I am sure. I am especially grateful to the Guernsey County Genealogical Society (Ohio), which provided much useful assistance.

The following people are those who I can identify who made what I will term significant contributions. Thank you.

Contributor's List – in alphabetical order – and there are many others…

Dorothy Adams
Don Baldwin
Sharon Barnes
Charles Braniger
Susie Bromley
Doug Carr
Mark Edick
Walter G. Elwell
Rebecca Fraas
Jet Hall
Lyle Jones
Mary Kinnick
Violet Lowe
E. Marsh
Evelyn L. McKittrick
Marcella Mickel
Bernadine Myers
Karen Nucci
Bernard Pitts
Stefanie Richardson
Juli Schwyhart
Sandi Share
Russell & Carolyn Stroud
Richard Tinkle
Maxine Trotter
Judith K. Vermilion
Dana Weedon
David Weise
Patricia Tebow Williams